Both Sides of Peace

Israeli and Palestinian
Political Poster Art

ISBN 1-885-449-04-6

This book is dedicated to Robert H. Bartelt and Floyd J. Helmick.

**This publication
was generously funded by
Gilbert Paper for The Friends of Gilbert Program**
Cover: Esse® White, Smooth, 80# Cover
Text: Esse® White, Smooth, 80# Text
**and
Meredith Webb Printing, Burlington, NC
Eyebeam, Morrisville, NC
Greg Plachta Photography, Durham, NC
Leo Adelman and Sandy Mayer
and
North Carolina Arts Council
United Arts Council of Raleigh and Wake County
and
The Arts and Culture Administration
Ministry of Education, Culture and Sports
Israel**

Published on the occasion
of an exhibition organized by the
Contemporary Art Museum,* Raleigh, North Carolina.
Opening date December 7, 1996. Opening sponsored by the
Raleigh Chapter of the American Institute of Graphic Arts and
The Gallery Group of the Contemporary Art Museum.
Curators: Dana Bartelt, New Orleans, LA,
Yossi Lemel, Tel Aviv, Israel,
Sliman Mansour, East Jerusalem, Israel,
and Fawzy El Emrany, Gaza City, Palestine.

*(formerly the City Gallery of Contemporary Art)

Dana Bartelt

Yossi Lemel

Fawzy El Emrany

Sliman Mansour

Both Sides of Peace

Israeli and Palestinian
Political Poster Art

Contemporary Art Museum, Raleigh, North Carolina

in association with

University of Washington Press, Seattle, Washington

Thou Shall Not Kill
Igael Tumarkin-Israeli

This poster was created in memory of Emil Greenzweig, Israeli peace activist who was killed during a peace demonstration.

Denise Dickens
Executive Director
Contemporary Art Museum

Acknowledgments

The power of art to move people, the power of knowledge to shape one's thoughts, and the power of understanding to create empathy for other's desires are truly great gifts to be used responsibly. It is the hope of the Contemporary Art Museum that a more in-depth understanding of the thoughts behind the posters will educate us about the views from both sides struggling for peace and co-existence. This provocative collection of Israeli and Palestinian political posters is in keeping with the Museum's tradition of stirring the viewer's awareness of present day issues. The balanced perspective represented in *Both Sides of Peace* was attained by the close collaboration between the curators—Dana Bartelt, an American graphic designer and professor at Loyola University New Orleans who has curated several major poster exhibitions including *Contemporary Czechoslovak Posters* for the Contemporary Art Museum and *Art as Activist: Revolutionary Posters of Central and Eastern Europe* for the Smithsonian Traveling Exhibition Service; Yossi Lemel, partner in the advertising firm Lemel Glaser Bar in Tel Aviv Israel, who has won many international awards for his advertising work and self-initiated political posters; Sliman Mansour, Director of the Al-Wasiti Art Centre in East Jerusalem and President of the League of Palestinian Artists, who has organized many exhibitions of Palestinian artists as well as joint Israeli/Palestinian shows abroad; and Fawzy El-Emrany, artist and art teacher from Gaza who has exhibited in Palestine, Israel and Europe.

It has been a great privilege and honor to again work closely with Dana Bartelt who brings a rigor and intensity to her scholarship and curatorial insights. Yossi Lemel gave North Carolina audiences much to think about as he presented talks to numerous groups during the opening of the exhibition and so generously shared his expertise with the graphic design community. Fawzy El Emrany worked tirelessly to coordinate the collection of works by artists from Gaza. Sliman Mansour's diligence in collecting works by Palestinian artists was invaluable.

Books have a life beyond the museum exhibition and in this case it was particularly important to involve writers alongside the graphic artists to characterize the shifting political current in the Middle East. We thank them for their contributions.

We are indebted to the lenders whose posters completed the comprehensive collection: the Palestinian Ministry of Culture—Fayez Sirsawi and Aser Sagga, Gaza; Roots Palestinian Youth Organization, Washington D.C.—Nabil Mohammad, Director; Harvard College Library, Judaica Division—Charles Berlin and Violet Gilboa; Harvard College Library, Middle East Division—Michael Hopper; Yale University Library—Simon Samoeil, David Tartakover, Israel; Anne Marie Oliver and Paul Steinberg, Cambridge, MA.

Sincere gratitude is extended to the generous contributors to the exhibition and catalog without whom the project would never have been realized: Gilbert Paper (Kathy Merckx), Meredith Webb Printing (Julia Zeigler), Eyebeam (Wiley Blackburn), Greg Plachta Photography, JW Labs, Typesthetics, Leo Adelman, Sandy Mayer, and The Arts and Culture Administration of the Ministry of Education, Culture and Sports, Israel.

The exhibition was made possible by support from Rechenbachs, Barefoot Press, Zubigraphics, Commercial Plastics, Alfredo Jarr, Paul Tesar, and Leo Adelman.

Special thanks to Sara Lemel, Nora Whisnant, Nick Hammer, Karla Hammer, Carol Leake, Naomi Nye, Aziz Shihab, David Simonton, Roger Cook and Daniel Russell. Thanks to Yossi Lemel for an outstanding exhibition poster design.

Members of the Raleigh Chapter of the American Institute of Graphic Arts gave their time, support and enthusiasm; in particular the Exhibition Committee members: Jessie Couch, President; Lisa Yow, Chair; Haig Khachatoorian, Pam Chastain, Cindy Anerdon, and Heather Hille.

The Contemporary Art Museum's Gallery Group served in many ways including a framing crew: Susan Benenson, Anne Sprinkle, Elizabeth Purrington, Bill Brown, Elana DeChurch, Caro Ealy, Cristina Favretto, Bill McEneaney, Stephanie Miller and Michael Reese.

A word of special thanks is due the Trustees and staff of the Contemporary Art Museum: Debbie Rives, former Chairman, Connie Shertz, Secretary, Frank Thompson, Chairman, Colette Waters, Curator of Exhibiitons and Education, Julia Waterfall, former Development Officer, Joey Howard, former Administrative Assistant and Preparator, and Sara Choi, curatorial intern.

We hope that *Both Sides of Peace* will provide a context for learning about a complex political and cultural situation that has troubled the Middle East for too long. The spirited creativity of the artists gives us food for thought and hope.

Contents

Independence Day
Tami Berger-Israeli
1988

Published in 1988 on the 1st anniversary of the Intifada and the 40th year of Israeli independence, this poster was banned by the Israeli government since it was illegal to show the Palestinian flag.

(following page)

Peace Agreement
Dan Reisinger-Israeli
1994

The signing of the Peace Agreement on the White House lawn between Israel and Jordan. Rabin, Peres and Arafat received the Nobel Peace Prize for their efforts for peace in the Middle East—a hopeful time.

חתימת חוזה השלום ישראל - ירדן, כ"א חשון תשנ"ה, 26 באוקטובר 1994

"אנו מושיטים יד לשלום ושכנות טובה..."
(מתוך מגילת העצמאות)

ראש הממשלה
رئيس الحكومة
Prime Minister

June 9, 1996

Dear Friends,

A new dawn, however hesitant, is slowly, gradually and irreversibly casting its light upon the Middle East. Not every corner of this vast geography is illuminated by it, but, whatever the setbacks, the long, cold black shadows of enmity and violence are irresistably fading before the rays of reconciliation, cooperation, coexistence and peace. We who fought each other for so long, we who inflicted suffering on each other for so long, we who buried our dead, those who fell in defense of that which we perceived to be utterly vital and precious- we have, in many instances, finally shaken hands. With some, we have even embraced. Not yet all. But I believe with all my heart that, eventually, we shall- all of us.

The hurdles are still many. We have a mountain of suspicion yet to negotiate. We have to find genuine solutions to an array of genuine conflicting interests. And we have to overcome fundamentalist fanaticism and inhumane terrorism perpetrated by evil-doers who cannot abide a future of Jewish-Arab reconciliation. Yet they, too, will retreat and perish in face of the new future dawn.

It is my belief that peace is the heart and soul of Judaism. It is the ancient heritage by which we have survived over the centuries against all logic and against all odds. I remain confident that Peace will prevail.

The exhibition of posters offers a graphic commentary of the opposing points of view of what is, surely, one of the most complex conflicts in the world. May it also offer a bridge of mutual respect- a bridge across which the respective sides may cross and encounter each other, no longer in acrimony but understanding.

To this goal, I have dedicated myself- to help construct this bridge of amity embodied in a rock of recognition that is solid. I believe it is.

Sincerely yours,

Shimon Peres

Shimon Peres

Jerusalem, Israel

Dana Bartelt

Both Sides of Peace

Dana Bartelt has curated several
poster exhibitions, including *Both
Sides of Peace* for the Contempo-
rary Art Museum and *Art as
Activist: Revolutionary Posters from
Central and Eastern Europe* for the
Smithsonian Traveling Exhibition
Service and has written many arti-
cles about poster design. She is
active in the American Institute of
Graphic Arts, and served as
President of the Raleigh/AIGA and
New Orleans Chapters. Professor
Bartelt teaches graphic design at
Loyola University New Orleans
and organizes a summer study in
Prague, Czech Republic, for North
Carolina State University School of
Design.

No More Victims
Dan Reisinger- Israeli
1993

The victims referred to in this
poster are both Israeli and Palestinian. The Israeli 'flag' is com-
posed of the Star of David and
two stripes. However, the traditional blue color of the Star of
David is replaced, in one portion,
with yellow, reminiscent of the
yellow star which Jews were
forced to wear during the Nazi
occupation of Europe. The other
portion is made of the red trian-
gle, and green and black stripes
taken from the Palestinian flag.

As I sat in the audience watching a slide presentation of posters by Israeli graphic designers Dan Reisinger and Yossi Lemel—I was impressed by the powerful, provocative images
shown on the screen. Yes, they were well designed—after all Dan Reisinger is an internationally acclaimed artist and Yossi Lemel is an award winning designer who had just
received the Silver Medal at the Brno Bienale—but the statements made by these posters
were what really impressed me. They didn't speak of Israel's rights to the land, the more
prevalent argument in the Middle East conflict; they pleaded for an end to the violence on
both sides (Reisinger's *No More Victims*) and showed empathy for another people's struggle for freedom (Lemel's *Happy Chanukah*). Reflecting on these images, I could not help
but wonder what Palestinian artists would say about these issues. In seeking the answer
to this question, I discovered an historical culture whose artistic expression also reveals a
deep sense of loss and yearning for peace. By presenting this collection to the American
public, I hope to share my understanding of Israeli and Palestinian peace-related art
through juxtaposition of the visual and written languages of both peoples.

The Israeli-Palestinian conflict continues to be the subject of editorial commentary and
media coverage in the United States. The names of Yasir Arafat, Yitzhak Rabin and Shimon
Peres are quite familiar to the American public now as were Moshe Dayan, Golda Meir,
and Anwar Sadat previously. Because of the endless reports of acts of war, occupation of
territories, and the plights of refugees and prisoners, many worry that the conflict will
never end. The issues as presented by the media sometimes seem all too simple while at
other times so complicated it appears to require a Ph.D. in Middle Eastern Studies to com-
prehend. From the beginning, we have all been subject to the biases of the press in deter-
mining what actually occurs in Israel and Palestine. However, as Amos Oz states in his
essay *The Israeli-Palestinian Conflict*, "...there is no basic misunderstanding between
Israelis and Palestinians; there is a very real conflict: they want the land because they think
it belongs to them...". The unexpected peace agreement signed in September 1993, the
importance of which was confirmed by the awarding of the Nobel Peace Prize to Arafat,
Rabin and Peres, gave new hope. Moderate Palestinians (the majority who elected Arafat
President of the Palestinian Authority) want peace—an end to occupation, poverty, and
confiscation of property. And, despite the assassination of Prime Minister Rabin, his
widow called on the many moderate Israelis and "peaceniks" to persevere in their struggle for a peace which would give all Israelis personal security and the right to live normal
lives free of fear. Although the Oslo peace agreement represented the desires of Palestinian
and Israeli moderates, rightwing extremists on both sides continue to thwart the peace
initiative.

In Israel the most visible statements regarding the peace process (other than mass media)
have been the posters found on hoardings, walls and kiosks and banners hanging on
balconies and windows. Many of these posters were produced by right wing groups pro-
claiming anti-peace sentiments. One depicted Rabin's face as a mask over Arafat's face, and

NO MORE VICTIMS

DAN REISINGER 3.9.93

another showed Arafat in a Nazi helmet. In March 1995, I was invited to give a presentation to the Israeli Graphic Designer's Association in Tel Aviv. Yossi Lemel, the Israeli co-curator of the exhibition, invited members to exhibit their political posters. Not too surprisingly, most designers and artists who participated were liberals, leftists, and/or pro-peace sympathizers. Many were critical of certain Israeli government actions against the Palestinians or expressed their frustration with the continuing bloodshed on both sides. In essence, they were sick of people dying and most major problems remaining unresolved.

I asked Israeli designers if their outspokenness had ever created problems with clients or resulted in government censorship. Most said 'no,' but Lemel cited a case when he designed a theater poster about a soldier being investigated for the killing of a Palestinian prisoner–*One of Us*. He used the particular green and red colors of the Palestinian flag and the theater made him change to less recognizable colors. The word 'Palestine' was also taboo. The poster *Independence Day* by Tami Berger, showing the Palestinian and Israeli flags tied together, was banned from public display by the Israeli government.

In 1988, a poster exhibition was organized in Israel to mark the 40th anniversary of its independence. Yarom Vardimon, an internationally acclaimed graphic designer, says of the exhibition, "...the works were more critical than praising, and more disturbing than exciting... The phenomenon of ugly and aggressive design, which connects pain and anger through cynicism and through efficient and simple tools, was at times almost revolutionary." The images that I found on most contemporary political posters were similarly dramatic and powerful. Many of the mostly photographic images employed layers of complex symbolism and yet, at first glance, appeared simple and straightforward. Vardimon noticed earlier that the sociopolitical undertakings in graphic design "generally critical, naturally deal with new and local symbols and their relationship to the culture's previous symbols. Symbols of Middle Eastern society's distress are pictures of bereavement, violence and religious rituals."

The varied references to 'old' and 'new' produce the multiple layers of meanings in the political poster. In David Tartakover's *Who Will Utter the Mighty Acts of Israel*, these layers are only discovered by those familiar with Israeli culture and Biblical history. The title is the opening to a children's festival song about the heroic Maccabee warriors. Although evoking the voices of children, the viewer is confronted by a woman in anguish over the presumed death of a loved one, perhaps a child. The cultural identity of the mother is ambiguous—she could be an Arab or a Jew. Further, the Hebrew word for 'heroism' is similar in sound pattern to the Hebrew word 'graves' suggesting an affinity between the two concepts. The line is also a transformation of the more ancient Biblical phrase 'Who will utter the mighty acts of the Lord.' Tartakover produced this poster following Israeli involvement in the Phalangist massacre of hundreds of Palestinians and Lebanese in the refugee camps of Sabra and Shatila. He is one of the most prolific poster artists in Israel, producing many self-initiated posters to express his political and social views. He has exhibited internationally in group and one-man exhibitions as well as in joint projects with Palestinian artists.

Judaic symbols are used extensively in Israel because it is a Jewish state. Most notable is the Star of David, also found on the Israeli flag. When the Star is shown in sky blue it refers to the flag and nation, when it appears in yellow, the reference is to the Holocaust when Nazis made Jews wear a yellow patch in the shape of the Star of David. The Holocaust is ever pre-

Who will utter the mighty acts of Israel?
David Tartakover- Israeli
1983

Produced after the massacres at Sabra and Shatila Refugee Camps, the multi-layered poster raises the question of responsibility. The cultural identity of the woman is ambiguous—Arab or Jewish? In Hebrew the word for 'mighty' is similar in sound to the word for 'graves' suggesting an affinity between the two concepts. The title is a refrain from a children's song about the Maccabees fight against the Greek invaders. It is used in ironic reference to the government's declaration of 1983 as the 'Year of Heroism' just as the Lebanon War entered its second year.

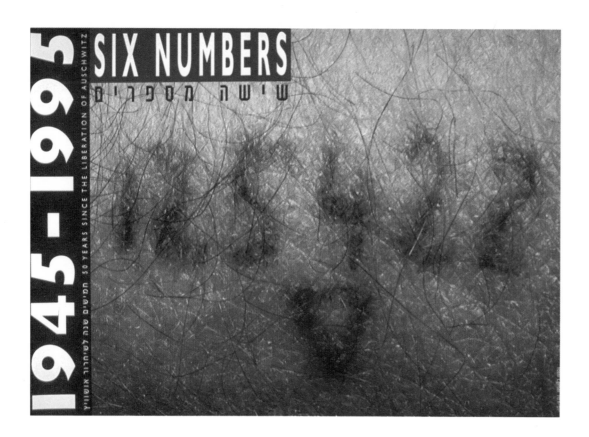

14

(opposite page)

Welcome
Yossi Lemel-Israeli
1991

The words 'welcome' are written in Hebrew and Amahari, the language of more than 15,000 Jewish Ethiopians evacuated on one night by Israelis in 1991. To lessen the possibility of 'losing' so many children, numbers were stuck to their foreheads to identify them. Even though it praises Israel's commitment to be refuge for all the Jews of the world, it is also cynical in the treatment of the people as cattle.

(opposite page)

Six Numbers
Yossi Lemel-Israeli
1995

Commemorating the liberation of Auschwitz (the numbers belong to the artist's father living in Israel), Mr. Lemel states that there are few families in Israel who were not touched by the Holocaust directly and that is a common thread amongst all. The 'six' also refers to the six million Jews murdered in the Holocaust.

Sweet Option
Yossi Lemel-Israeli
1994

The Star of David is made from a baklava, a Middle Eastern sweet cake, placed on an Arab plate. It refers to a political idea settling the debate between Jordan and Israel (The Jordan Option) which was introduced by Igal Alon, then Foreign Minister, but was never realized.

האופציה המתוקה
תשנ״ה

sent in the psyche of the nation. Lemel's father survived the concentration camp at Auschwitz, although many of his family did not. His poster *Six Numbers*, which commemorates the 50 years since the liberation of Auschwitz in 1945, is simply and powerfully an image of the six numbers tattooed onto the arm of his father. The number six also refers to his six family members and the six million Jews exterminated by the Nazis in World War II. Lemel says, "I wanted to show that the numbers were on real flesh, a human being. I used color and enlarged it to burn it into your memory as it was burned into their flesh." He also says, "The Holocaust is like a thread that weaves through the entire culture...after what happened in Europe, to my family, it was hard to believe in human nature and not to want to be vindictive, but during my school years I began to realize that 'they' are not all devils and I began my mission to be more just and fight against racism. And now when I teach, I assign topics dealing with justice, racism, domestic violence, and religious tolerance to my students—rather than consumer issues." Along similar lines, Amos Oz notes in his essay *The Israeli Palestinian Conflict*, "...some victims of oppression and discrimination and racism indeed become more tolerant, more receptive, more sensitive to the sufferings of others. Whereas other victims of the same horrible experience tend to become more vindictive, more angry and more suspicious. Both these contradicting responses are equally human. They may not be equally humane but equally human."

One of Israel's basic tenets is the in-gathering of the exiled ancient tribes of Israel who were scattered around the world. Four out of five Israelis are Jewish. Many are Ashkenazi Jews from Europe who immigrated in large numbers (*aliyahs*) after the Nazi Holocaust. Israel continues to accept immigrants, with recent *aliyahs* from Russia and Ethiopia. The dramatic influx of hundreds of thousands of these immigrants has resulted in cultural and political change. In an already crowded land, the new immigrants provided Israel justification for the rapid growth of controversial settlements in the West Bank. Lemel's poster *Welcome* reveals the ambivalence among Israelis toward the arrival, in 1991 of 20,000 Ethiopian Jews who were airlifted to Israel during a secret overnight operation. "So they wouldn't get lost," Lemel noted, "the children, like cattle, were marked with numbers on their foreheads." Lemel and photographer Israel Cohen took the picture of four children with their actual numbers forming '1991.' The word 'welcome' is in both Hebrew and Amahari, the Ethiopian language.

Israeli artists produce primarily western style political posters (large format and photographic techniques). It was with similar expectation that I started searching for Palestinian political posters. Sliman Mansour, President of the League of Palestinian Artists in Arab East Jerusalem quickly set me straight regarding what I would find, what I wouldn't, what Palestinians considered posters and what it was like for a Palestinian artist to live in Israel and the Occupied Territories. A confirmation of what I was to learn was not long in coming. During my first visit to Israel I met with both Israeli and Palestinian peace activists to collect materials regarding the peace movement. Upon my second visit, I was singled out among all the passengers boarding my El Al (Israeli airline) flight for an intensive 2 hour interrogation. My computer (with all the research for this project) was confiscated and I was roughly shoved onto the plane. It was a frightening and humiliating experience.

JERUSALEM

Jerusalem
Shlomi Gold-Israeli
1995

The symbols in the word
'Jerusalem' represent the three
monotheistic religions all in one
city: Christianity, Islam and
Judaism The poster was created
for Jerusalem's 3000th anniversary and, as the artist states, "to
express hope for peace for all
and to promote understanding,
tolerance and brotherhood, to
dream a dream of Jerusalem
which is home to everyone,
every belief, every culture. One
for all and all in one-Jerusalem."

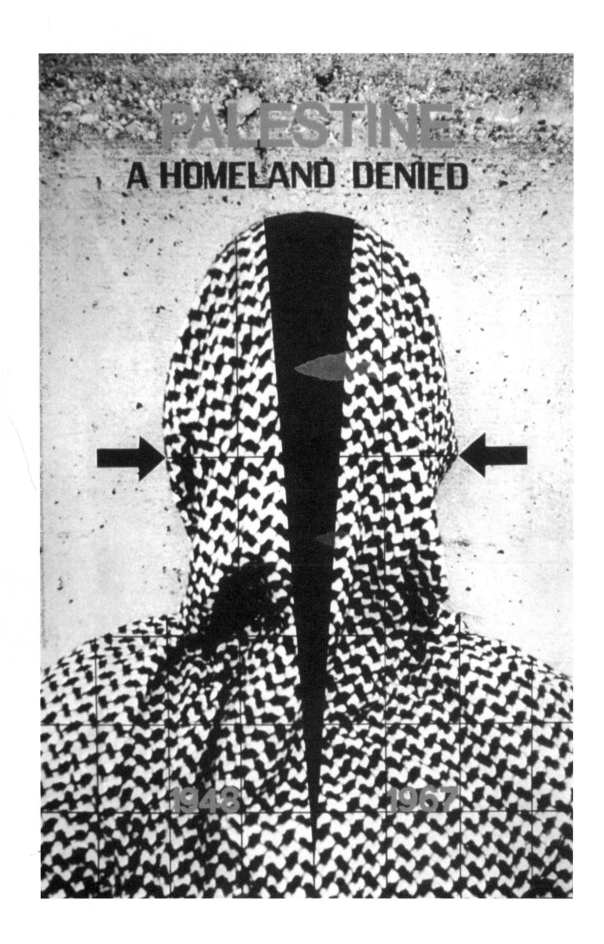

Palestine A Homeland Denied
Artist unknown
1988
(from the collection of David Tartakover)

This poster was produced for an exhibition organized in Iraq in support of the return of the land to the Palestinians. Participants included artists from around the world.

Political Zionism, which began in the late 19th century, called for the formation of a national Jewish homeland in Palestine; a land where Palestinian Arabs constituted the overwhelming majority of the population. With the rise of Nazism in Europe, the need for a Jewish refuge became urgent and the powers of Europe and the Americas supported the Zionist cause. The events surrounding the formation of the state of Israel and the displacement of the Palestinians are briefly summarized in the Timeline. They are too complex to do justice in the present context. Yet, one of the most fundamental issues in understanding the Palestinians' continuing struggle for recognition as a nation with political and human rights concerns the question of how one builds a national home for one people in a land inhabited by another. As expressed by Edward Said (*The Question of Palestine*), "We were on the land; were our dispossession and our effacement, by which almost a million of us were made to leave Palestine and our society made nonexistent, justified even to save the remnant of European Jews that had survived Nazism? By what moral or political standard are we expected to lay aside our claims to our national existence, our land, our human rights?" The 'right to the land' ideologies hold many Palestinians and Israelis captive and threaten to bury the future in the past. Other critical issues for both peoples include personal security and safe national boundaries. These issues provide radicals on both sides justification for further territorial expansion and militant actions. Alternatively, those seeking peace have attempted to accommodate these issues by focusing on ending the conflict through political concessions.

Amos Oz has suggested that secure national boundaries for both Israelis and Palestinians should precede reconciliation in a manner similar to the relatively good relations eventually established among European countries, Israel and Germany following World War II. Another component of peaceful coexistence also includes mutual respect. While both sides engage in deprecatory language against each other, negative stereotyping of Palestinian Arabs is used effectively by rightwing Israelis (aided by militant Palestinian groups' activities) and willingly spread by the media in the United States. Said deplores the use of 'poisonous and dehumanizing rhetoric' used by some Israeli government officials and intellectuals to "characterize all Palestinian acts of resistance as terrorist and Palestinians as nonhuman..." While the horrific bombings by Palestinian extremists are widely publicized, the number of Palestinians killed and wounded exceeds the number of Israelis by a factor of 10 to 1 by some estimates. The number of Palestinians imprisoned and deported, the number of Palestinian homes demolished and the loss of human rights are also rarely reported in the media. Said notes "the discrepancy is both great and greatly unadmitted." In the United States, a land where human rights and freedom of speech are most touted, pro-Palestinian sentiments are virtually taboo and condescension, at best, the norm. In this framework art is one of the most effective antidotes to prejudice and dehumanizing stereotypes; allowing both sides to see, in all its complexity, each other's very real and human pain.

In December 1987, young Palestinians living in the Territories, angry at the Israelis who had humiliated and exploited them, their exiled leaders and the Arab World who had abandoned them, revolted. The uprising which took place is known as the "intifada", which means "shaking off" in Arabic. The Palestinians were armed with stones, anger and despair. It became clear to many Israelis that the occupation was intolerable and that neither the suffering nor the national aspirations of the Palestinians could be ignored. The effects of the 1987 intifada were boundless. It was an uprising not only of a people in revolt,

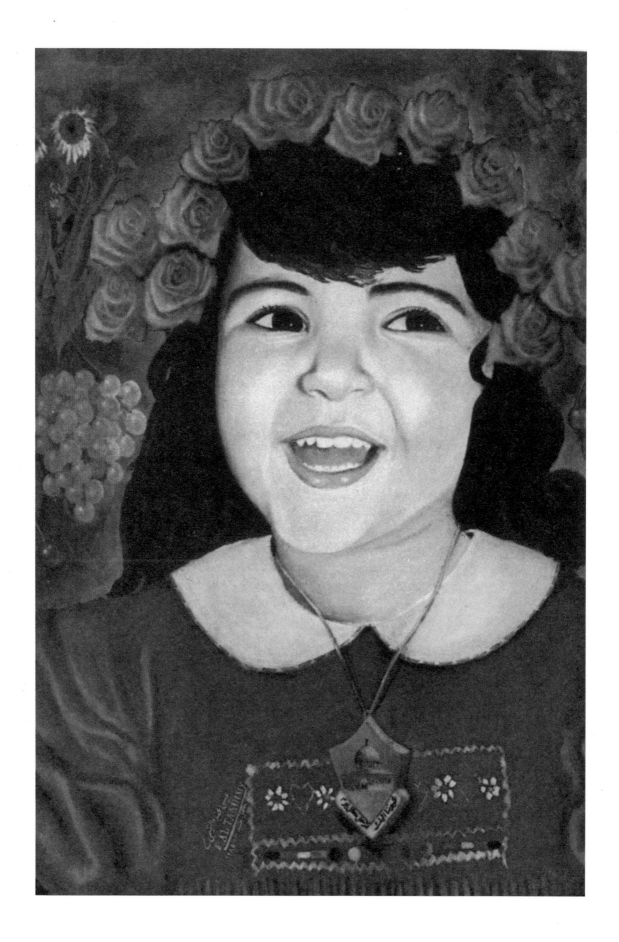

but an uplifting of spirit and a time of inspiration for Palestinian artists. According to Taleb Dweik and Sliman Mansour the intifada brought great changes to the expressions of artists, filling them with courage to paint in a new bold way. Images of fighters on powerful stallions appeared—a vision of hope and strength characteristic of the intifada for the Palestinian people. Mansour worked with many other artists to keep Palestinian artistic traditions alive and flourishing, even under oppressive conditions. These included the fear of imprisonment for creating any nationalistic images deemed subversive by the Israeli government, the banning of travel outside the Occupied Territories, and lack of materials. Many artists turned to indigenous materials, earth, clay, etc. and made their palettes from the pistils of flowers. Not being able to travel outside the Occupied Territories created a sense of both physical and creative isolation. Many of the artists have not been allowed to accompany their shows to other countries, while others have had their works confiscated from exhibitions within the Territories. Mansour organized exhibitions (both within and outside the Territories) and later established the Al-Wasiti Art Centre in East Jerusalem to promote growth and exposure in the arts.

The Visitor
Issa Abeido-Palestinian

Many 'posters' created by Palestinian artists were paintings turned into posters and postcards. The girl in the painting is the daughter of a Palestinian prisoner. Without being overtly political, Palestinians value these images as reminders of those imprisoned or detained in Israeli prisons. She wears a pendant with a picture of the Dome of the Rock and the grapes denote that she comes from Hebron.

Sliman Mansour showed me 'posters' which are reproductions of paintings that superficially appear to be passive pictures of domestic life—women in traditional Palestinian embroidered dresses, children reading their lessons, and a mother embracing her children. These are all symbols of a tradition and national pride which they feel the Israelis have tried to destroy. The mother represents Palestine, and her children, the people of Palestine; the reading lessons refer to refugee camps where no schooling is provided. The poster, *The Visitor*, an innocent-looking painting of a smiling Palestinian girl, is a reminder of the Palestinian prisoners who were deprived of being with their families. Some posters were so popular that Israeli soldiers found them on routine house searches, and, knowing their significance, confiscated them. One of the most popular posters, by Sliman Mansour, *Carry On*, is of an old man carrying Jerusalem on his back. Jerusalem is one of the actual and symbolic sacred centers of the Islamic religion—as well as of Christianity and Judaism. Mansour was arrested by Israeli soldiers at the Jordanian border for possession of this 'subversive' poster.

Many of the paintings have hidden symbols through metaphor or vague reference, because any blatant portrayals of anti-Israeli images or pro-Palestinian independence could result in arrest. Objects such as the Palestinian flag and its colors, the word 'Palestine' were all banned and their use was punishable, as was as any reference to the PLO. Similarly, the kaffiyah, the red and white or black and white head scarf worn by Arabic men, most notably by Yasir Arafat, has a pattern which is immediately identified. Naturally, all posters produced underground or outside the Occupied Territories employed these symbols freely. The Dome of the Rock, a mosque built in 640 A.D. in Jerusalem also stands as a symbol of unity amongst the Palestinian people. This image is seen in theater, political and peace posters.

Fawzy El Emrany and Taysir Batniji are self-trained graphic designers. Their poster *Peace for Us, Peace for the World*, is reminiscent of the traditional decorative calligraphy seen on the graphic store signs in the streets of Gaza and other Arab cities. This particular poster uses only one color, but many of the Palestinian posters use a rich kaleidoscope of colors also found in the elaborate works of embroidered Palestinian dresses and ancient and contemporary mosaics with intricate geometric patterns.

Almost all of the PLO posters were produced outside the Occupied Territories, many by Palestinian artists living in exile or by artists of other nationalities sympathetic to the Palestinian cause. A 1988 exhibition held in Iraq entitled *A Homeland Denied* included posters by artists from around the world. About two thirds of the Palestinian people live outside Israel and the Occupied Territories. Posters produced by artists in exile often speak of the longing to return to their country and the pain of the loss of family, home and homeland. Nabil Mohammad, director of Roots in Washington, D.C., was born in a refugee camp in Lebanon. Although he has lived in Washington for 12 years he continues to "dream to touch the soil of Palestine." This is the main issue for the Palestinian people —to be recognized as a nation with the right to return to their land. (To many Jews this may sound hauntingly familiar.)

Posters produced within the Occupied Territories prior to 1994 are almost impossible to find. Small format posters, usually produced on photo copiers and hand colored, were pasted on walls overnight and scraped off the next morning by Israeli patrols. The artists are unknown, of course, since identification would have led to certain arrest. These posters were commemorative of an anniversary of a significant event such as Land Day, Day of the Child, Martyr's Day or the establishment of a political party or movement like the PLO. The walls of Gaza and the West Bank are still covered with the faces of the many young fighters who died in their struggle for independence.

Because material was scarce and printing shops forbidden, young Palestinians took to painting the walls with revolutionary slogans and images. The walls became the canvasses for their 'posters.' Israeli soldiers were allowed to shoot at those painting graffiti on the walls; Mansour told me that a youth was shot and killed while writing the word 'peace' on a wall. Many of the vibrant murals are pictorial documents recording the events of the intifada, and while the artists remain anonymous, their party affiliation is known through coded color—black for the Fateh Party, green for Islamic movements, and red for the socialist parties. These are simple codes which are easily translatable; other symbols are more complex and depend on the viewer's knowledge for their translations.

To an Israeli, a Palestinian with his head wrapped in a kaffiyah is a rock throwing *shebab* or even a 'terrorist', something quite threatening—to a Palestinian, he is the symbol of revolution and resistance, a hero, a martyr. To a Palestinian, a young Israeli soldier is potentially an assassin, a gun-happy bully, a destroyer of family and home—to an Israeli, he or she is part of the tough disciplined Israeli Defense Force that has risked his/her life for the protection of the Jewish State. These images are formed from individual or collective experiences and perspectives. The way we as Americans interpret the images and events of the Middle East is almost entirely based on news media coverage, and on the icons and symbols that are part of our vocabularies and cultures. Speaking of Yasir Arafat (Abu Ammar), Hanan Ashrawi states in her book *This Side of Peace*, "I saw the side of Abu Ammar that was not visible through television or print reports. The western media refused to look beyond the image and he was reduced to outlines rather than substance...it was much easier for the west to deal with Abu Ammar as an archetypal terrorist, a villain and a revolutionary leader ...This one dimensional image of bogeyman was taken as representative of all Palestinians." She also says of her college experience in the United States, "...as soon as people realized I was not going to jump up and start belly dancing between the salad and main course, nor was I going to toss a grenade into the dessert, I began to make friends."

**Omar Mahmud al-Qassaem
artist unknown-Palestinian
1991**
(from the collection of Anne Marie Oliver and Paul Steinberg)

Omar Mahmud al-Qassaem, a leader of the Democratic Front for the Liberation of Palestine (DFLP), was captured in the late 1960's and after 20 years in prison died there in 1989. He is referred to as the 'Mandela of Palestine' and his elaborate grave in Jerusalem is a place of pilgrimage. This poster commemorates the second anniversary of his death. On his face is superimposed a blood red sun, whose rays nourish a green stalk of wheat, a sacrificial image. The meaning is doubled by the slogan: "A thousand flowers for the one who wove the fabric of the homeland from his veins."

الفـن زهـرة مـن أكمـام الوطـن بـروق

الذكـرى السـنويـة الثامـنة لاسـتشهـاد القائـد الوطـني الرمـز

الشهيـد عمر محمـود القاسـم

Typical grafitti found on the walls all over Gaza depicting the mostly youthful martyrs of the intifada and slogans from different political factions—in red, the communist party—in black, the Fateh party and in green, the HAMAS.

24

In December 1996 the opening for the exhibition of this poster collection was scheduled at the City Gallery of Contemporary Art in Raleigh, N.C. Co-curators Fawzy El Emrany and Yossi Lemel were invited to attend and speak about the Palestinian and Israeli posters respectively. Despite numerous requests to the US Consulate and calls to Senator Jessie Helms, Mr. El Emrany, a university educated artist and peace advocate, was denied a visa to enter the USA to speak at the opening. According to a U.S. Consulate official, entry was denied because he was a single Palestinian male.

Biases and prejudices are easily formed through ignorance of cultural beliefs, style and languages. Vardimon feels that, "the multitude of cultures and languages in this tiny country [Israel] makes it an ideal laboratory for dealing with questions of visual communication... sociopolitical messages as a daily routine." With such a diverse citizenry comes a diversity of written languages—Hebrew, Arabic, Russian, Ethiopian, English and even Vietnamese—all with their own written alphabets. Yossi Lemel observes that, "the Arab culture is totally separate (from ours) especially from the European and American Jews—we are less familiar with their icons and symbols". Historically, Palestinians have almost always been represented rather than spoken to, and it is enlightening to learn how they represent themselves.

Over the years many Israelis and Palestinians (including those who have lost loved ones to the struggle) have reached out to each other in peace. Perhaps the best known Israeli peace organization is 'Peace Now' which was formed by Israeli army reservists who had seen the trauma of occupation—both to the Palestinians and to the Israeli soldiers who had to enforce it. However, following the assassination of Prime Minister Rabin it appears that the voices of peace have been subdued. In the United States there appears to be continued interest in a peaceful resolution to the Middle East Conflict. Pulitzer prize winning journalists, such as Glenn Frankel and Thomas Friedman, have written frank accounts of political events in the Middle East and text books have begun to present the history of the area from both perspectives.

This collection is intended to bring the different voices of the cultures involved in the Middle East Conflict to the attention of an American audience in written and pictorial form—to see them, learn from them and hopefully begin to understand them. This collection is not simply about Jews and Arabs and it is not about right or wrong. It is about a passionate and desperate desire of all people to live in peace, to grow and to flourish, and to be allowed to raise their children with pride and joy.

Hanan Ashrawi

Speech at the Madrid Peace Conference

31 October 1991

We, the people of Palestine, stand before you in the fullness of our pain, our pride, and our anticipation, for we long harbored a yearning for peace and a dream of justice and freedom. For too long, the Palestinian people have gone unheeded, silenced and denied. Our identity negated by political expediency; our right for struggle against injustice maligned; and our present existence subdued by the past tragedy of another people. For the greater part of this century we have been victimized by the myth of a land without a people and described with impunity as the invisible Palestinians. Before such willful blindness, we refused to disappear or to accept a distorted identity. Our intifada is a testimony to our perseverence and resilience waged in a just struggle to regain our rights. It is time for us to narrate our own story, to stand witness as advocates of truth which has long lain buried in the consciousness and conscience of the world. We do not stand before you as supplicants, but rather as the torch bearers who know that, in our world of today, ignorance can never be an excuse. We seek neither an admission of guilt after the fact, nor vengeance for past inequities, but rather an act of will that would make a just peace a reality.

The Palestinian people are one, fused by centuries of history in Palestine, bound together by a collective memory of shared sorrows and joys, and sharing a unity of purpose and vision. Our songs and ballads, full of tales and children's stories, the dialect of our jokes, the image of our poems, that hint of melancholy which colors even our happiest moments, are as important to us as the blood ties which link our families and clans. Yet, an invitation to discuss peace, the peace we all desire and need, comes to only a portion of our people. It ignores our national, historical, and organic unity. We come here wrenched from our sisters and brothers in exile to stand before you as the Palestinians under occupation, although we maintain that each of us represents the rights and interests of the whole.

And Jerusalem, ladies and gentlemen, that city which is not only the soul of Palestine, but the cradle of three world religions, is tangible even in its claimed absence from our midst at this stage. It is apparent, through artificial exclusion from this conference, that this is a denial of its right to seek peace and redemption. For it, too, has suffered from war and occupation. Jerusalem, the city of peace, has been barred from a peace conference and deprived of its calling. Palestinian Jerusalem, the capital of our homeland and future state, defines Palestinian existence, past, present, and future, but itself has been denied a voice and an identity. Jerusalem defies exclusive possessiveness or bondage. Israel's annexation of Arab Jerusalem remains both clearly illegal in the eyes of the world community, and an affront to the peace that this city deserves.

We come to you from a tortured land and a proud, though captive people, having been asked to negotiate with our occupiers, but leaving behind the children of the intifada, and a people under occupation and under curfew who enjoined us not to surrender or forget. As we speak, thousands of our brothers are languishing in Israeli prisons and detention camps, most detained without evidence, charge or trial, many cruelly mistreated and tortured in interrogation, guilty only in seeking freedom or daring to defy the occupation. We speak in their name and we say: Set them free. As we speak, the tens of thousands who have been wounded or permanently disabled are in pain. Let peace

Hanan Mikhail-Ashrawi, founder of the Palestinian Independent Commission for Citizens' Rights, former spokesperson for the leadership of the Palestinians in the Occupied Territories, and professor of English at Birzeit University in the West Bank, is now Minister of Higher Education for the Palestinian Authority. She is author of the book *This Side of Peace: A Personal Account*.

Martyrs Day
artist unknown-Palestinian
1979
(from the collection of Roots, Palestinian Youth Organization, Washington D.C.)

The shape of what used to be Palestine is made of figures of martyrs that gave their lives in the struggle to reclaim the land.

heal their wounds. As we speak, the eyes of thousands of Palestinian refugees, deportees, and displaced persons since 1967 are haunting us, for exile is a cruel fate. Bring them home. They have the right to return. As we speak, the silence of demolished homes echoes through the halls and in our minds. We must rebuild our homes in our free state.

And what do we tell the loved ones of those killed by army bullets? How do we answer the questions and the fear in our children's eyes? For one out of three Palestinian children under occupation has been killed, injured, or detained in the past four years. How can we explain to our children that they are denied education, for schools are so often closed by the army? Or why their life is in danger for raising a flag in a land where even children are killed or jailed? What requiem can be sung for trees uprooted by army bulldozers? And most of all, who can explain to those whose lands are confiscated and clear waters stolen, a message of peace? Remove the barbed wire. Restore the land and its life-giving water. The settlements must stop now. Peace cannot be waged while Palestinian land confiscated in myriad ways and the status of occupied territories is being decided each day by Israeli bulldozers and barbed wire. This is not simply a position. It is an irrefutable reality. Territory for peace is a travesty when territory for illegal settlement is official Israeli policy and practice. The settlements must stop now.

In the name of the Palestinian people, we wish to directly address the Israeli people with whom we have had a prolonged exchange of pain: Let us share hope, instead. We are willing to live side by side on the land and the promise of the future. Sharing, however, requires two partners, willing to share as equals. Mutuality and reciprocity must replace domination and hostility for genuine reconciliation and coexistence under international legality. Your security and ours are mutually dependent, as entwined as the fears and nightmares of our children. We have seen some of you at your best and at your worst. For the occupier can hide no secrets from the occupied, and we are witness to the toll that occupation has exacted from you and yours.

We have seen you agonize over the transformation of your sons and daughters into instruments of a blind and violent occupation. And we are sure that at no time did you envisage such a role for the children whom you thought would forge your future. We have seen you look back in deepest sorrow at the tragedy of your past, and you look in horror at the disfigurement of the victim-turned-oppressor. Not for this have you nurtured your hopes, dreams, and your off-spring. This is why we have responded with solemn appreciation to those of you who came to offer consolation to our bereaved, to give support to those whose homes were being demolished and to extend encouragement and counsel to those detained behind barbed wire and iron bars. And we have marched together, often choking together in the nondiscriminatory tear gas or crying out in pain as the clubs descended on both Palestinian and Israeli alike, for pain knows no national boundaries, and no one can claim a monopoly on suffering. We once formed a human chain around Jerusalem, joining hands and calling for peace. Let us today form a moral chain around Madrid and continue that noble effort for peace and a promise of freedom for our sons and daughters. Break through the barriers of mistrust and manipulated fears. Let us look forward in magnanimity and in hope.

To our people in exile and under occupation, who have sent us to this appointment, laden with their trust, love, aspirations, we say that the load is heavy and the task is great, but we shall be true. In the words of our great national poet Mahmud Darwish: My homeland is not a suitcase, and I am no traveler.

To the exiled and the occupied we say you shall return and you shall remain and we will prevail, for our cause is just. We will put on our embroidered robes and kaffiyahs in the sight of the world and celebrate together on the day of liberation.

Palestine Needs Your Love
artist unknown-Palestinian
(from the collection of the Middle East Division of the Harvard College Library)

A cry for help to the world.

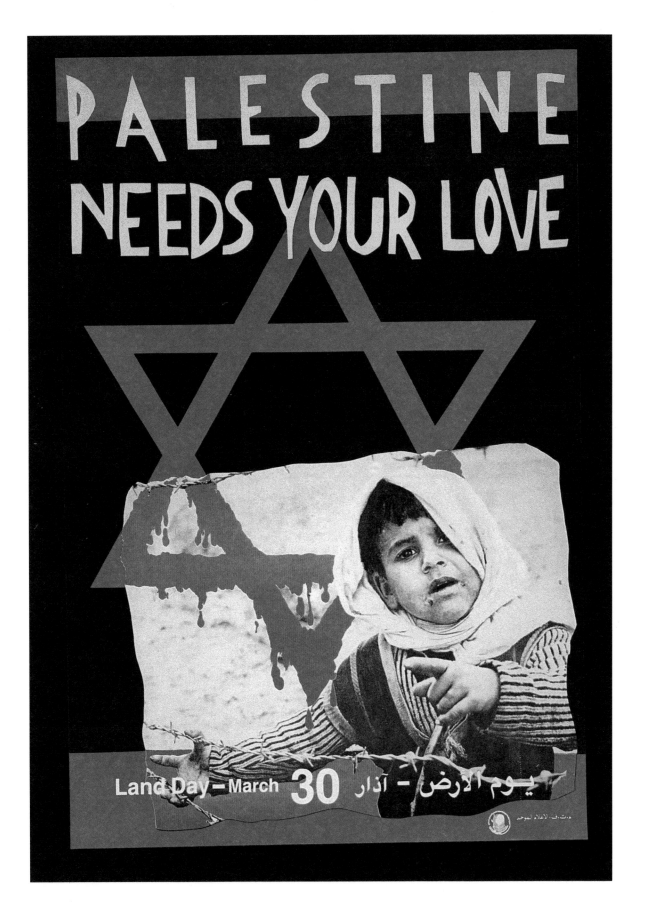

1 November 1991

Ladies and gentlemen, the issue is land. And what is at stake here is the survival of the Palestinian people on what is left of our olive groves and orchards, our terraced hills and peaceful valleys, our ancestral homes, villages, and cities. International legitimacy demands the restoration of the illegally occupied Arab and Palestinian lands to their rightful owners. Israel must recognize the concept of limits—political, legal, moral, and territorial—and must decide to join the community of nations by accepting the terms of international law and the will of the international community.

No amount of circumlocution or self-deception can alter the fact. Security can never be obtained through the acquisition of other people's territory, and geography is not the criterion for security. The opposite is actually true. Retaining or expanding occupied territory is one sure way of perpetuating hostility and resentment. We are offering the Israeli people a unique chance for genuine security through peace. Only by solving the real grievances and underlying causes of instability and conflict can genuine and long-standing stability and security be obtained.

We the people of Palestine hereby offer the Israelis an alternative path to peace and security: Abandon mutual fear and mistrust; approach us as equals; within a two-state solution; and let us work for the development and prosperity of our region based on mutual benefit and well-being. We have already wasted enough time, energy, and resources locked in this violent embrace of mutual destruction and defensiveness. We urge you to take this opportunity and rise to meet the challenge of peace.

Palestinians are a people with legitimate national rights. We are not the inhabitants of territories, or an accident of history, or an obstacle to Israeli expansionists, or an abstract demographic problem. You may wish to close your eyes to this fact, but we are here in the sight of the world, before your very eyes. And we shall not be denied. In exile or under occupation, we are one people, united despite adversity, determined to exercise our right to self-determination and to establish an independent state led by our own legitimate and acknlowledged leadership.

To the cosponsors and to the international community that seeks the achievement of a just peace in the Middle East, you have given us a fair hearing and for that we thank you.We, the people of Palestine, stand before you in the fullness of our pain, our pride, and our anticipation, for we long harbored a yearning for peace and a dream of justice and freedom. For too long, the Palestinian people have gone unheeded, silenced and denied. Our identity negated by political expediency; our right for struggle against injustice maligned; and our present existence subdued by the past tragedy of another people. For the greater part of this century we have been victimized by the myth of a land without a people and described with impunity as the invisible Palestinians. Before such willful blindness, we refused to disappear or to accept a distorted identity. Our intifada is a testimony to our perseverance and resilience waged in a just struggle to regain our rights. It is time for us to narrate our own story, to stand witness as advocates of truth which has long lain buried in the consciousness and conscience of the world. We do not stand before you as supplicants, but rather as the torch bearers who know that, in our world of today, ignorance can never be an excuse. We seek neither an admission of guilt after the fact, nor vengeance for past inequities, but rather an act of will that would make a just peace a reality.

Land day March 30
artist unknown-Palestinian
(from the collection of the Middle East Division of the Harvard College Library)

A take-off of the popular American magazine Life, the artist, showing a youth with a slingshot, suggests that the life of the Palestinians is to fight for freedom.

Land Day – March **30**   يـوم الأرض – آذار

INTIFADA

PALESTINIAN

The Flower is a Flower
Adnan Zubaidy-Palestinian

The poppy, an international symbol of revolution, represents Palestine with its roots embedded in the soil. It is said that the poppy gets its red color from the blood of the martyrs spilled into the ground. Even though this poster was created to promote education, the colors used—red, black, green and white—the same as the Palestinian flag and the symbolic meanings turn it into a political message.

(opposite page)

Visit Palestine
Franz Kraus
1936
(from the collection of David Tartakover)

This reproduction of an old travel poster was reproduced by artist David Tartakover to remind us that the land known to us today as Israel was once Palestine.

Roots
Ben-Ami Ratinsky- Israeli
1991

The artists states, "Some say that Israel is ephemeral. But I say Israel is deeply rooted for thousands of years and will stay here forever."

David Ben Gurion
David Tartakover- Israeli

The silhouette of David Ben Gurion, first Prime Minister of Israel wears a blue patch for Israel, not the yellow patch of the Holocaust.

 חדש

New
Zvi Levin-Israeli
1994

Hundreds of thousands of Russian Jews emigrated to Israel (called the aliyah) with hopes of a new life, but many found themselves unwelcome and without work. Many new settlements were established in the Occupied Territories to accommodate the new residents, which furthered tensions between Israel and Palestine.

(Opposite page)

I.....and you? We are all immigrants.
Raphael Adato-Israeli
1994

The poster starts with the line "I was born...." and continues to tell a story of a typical Israeli family whose roots reach back to Eastern Europe, whose friends come from Turkey and so on. Even though Israel is a 'melting pot' of Jews and non-Jews from all over the world, some recent immigrants are being discriminated against by Israelis who were born in Israel. The artist raises the question that we (Israelis) are all immigrants and should not discriminate. The cactus or 'sabra' represents the native Israeli.

נולדתי באוסטריה
ועליתי לארץ בשנת 1970. אבי הוא
יליד תל–אביב והוריו עלו מתורכיה
בשנות השלושים. אמי היא ילידת
יוגוסלביה, שגדלה באוסטריה.
אשתי נולדה בישראל. גם הוריה
הם ילידי הארץ. הוריהם נולדו
ברוסיה ובגליציה, וסבתא אחת
היגרה עם משפחתה לארגנטינה
לפני המלחמה. יש לי חבר שהוריו
הם ממרוקו. אבל שם המשפחה
שלהם הוא שם רוסי; הסבא
שלו היה דיפלומט רוסי ששרת
במרוקו. אשתו של החבר עלתה
מדנמרק. הם הכירו בארצות הברית.

העולים זה אנחנו!

Amos Oz

At the Bridge

Amos Oz, an Israeli author, essayist and activist for peace, has written 15 books translated into 29 languages, and has been the recipient of many major literary awards. He holds a Chair in Modern Hebrew Literature at Ben-Gurion University of the Negev, Beer-Sheva and has been awarded three honorary doctorates. Oz has been a leading figure with the Israeli Peace Movement including 'Peace Now" since its beginning in 1977. He lives in Arad in the Negev Desert in southern Israel with his family.

Peace No U-turn
Zvi Rosenberg-Israeli
1995

The artist expresses his indication that there is no alternative than to continue forward towards peace.

The Israeli-Arab war has been going on now for almost three generations. It began with sporadic attacks by the Arabs on the Jews returning to their homeland. Later it escalated into a vicious circle of belligerence, extending all the way from Iran to North Africa. Tens of thousands of Israelis have been killed and maimed; and over one hundred thousand Arabs. In the beginning it was no more than a feud between neighbors, involving knives and handguns. Eventually it deteriorated into a war of tanks and planes and ballistic missiles. With the Gulf War, just two years ago, it reached new thresholds, verging on apocalyptic means of mass destruction, at the same time becoming once again a battle of knives and stones.

Hate-filled fanatics have always attempted to turn this conflict into a religious war, a race war, a war between every Jew and every Arab, as are those wars in Ireland and Bosnia. But the fact is that the conflict between ourselves and the Palestinians is not a holy war but essentially a battle of two people, both of whom regard this country as their one and only homeland: that tragic clash between right and right.

For decades now, we proposed to the Arabs one compromise after another; including compromises which were much harder for us than the one which is now being negotiated. But the enemy rejected any compromise and persistently demanded that the Jews dismember their state and go away. This was a blunt, cruel attitude which we and they paid for in rivers of blood and an abyss of suffering. The Israeli victory in the 1967 Six Day War was followed by some euphoric years, during which our governments refused to recognize the very existence of the Palestinian people, expecting the Palestinians to forget their national identity and to surrender to our domination over every inch of the land. This Israeli policy was both immoral and unrealistic. And now we have all reached a crossroads: the two peoples are finally about to come to terms with the simple fact that they are two peoples and that, for both of them, the country is their homeland. We and they- along with most of the Arab world- are ready now to consider a partition of the land between its peoples. What partition and under what conditions- this question still involves a complex process of bargaining: who gets what and how much and under what terms, and how to ensure Israel's peace and security after the termination of the Israeli occupation of the West Bank and the Gaza Strip. All this must be clarified around the negotiating table, and calls for wisdom, patience and vision. Clearly, in this compromise, the Palestinians are going to get parts of the land, whereas we get documents and promises, and it is therefore crucial that an element of time is included in the equation, so that Israel has time to go to the bank, to make sure that the Arab peace check does not bounce. This means that between the agreement and the actual completion of the Israeli withdrawal, some years will have to elapse. In the meantime we will have to hold on to certain positions which will enable us to cancel the deal in case it turns out that the Palestinians are unwilling or unable to deliver their part of the bargain.

In 1947 the United Nations General Assembly resolved to partition the land between its two peoples, along geographic lines which today no Israeli would accept and no reasonable Palestinian would claim. That resolution provided the legal foundation for the establishment of Israel. Palestine, on the other hand, did not come into being in 1947, among other reasons because regular Arab armies from neighboring countries occupied territories designated for a Palestinian state. It might be equally embarrassing for Palestinians and Israelis to recall now that, in 1947, whereas Palestine had not been recognized by any nation, not even by Arab nations, not even by the Palestinians themselves who made no attempt to establish their own sovereignty- Israel, and Israel alone, did recognize the Palestinians: it did so in its very Declaration of Independence, proposing at the same time peace and friendly neighborliness.

Now, at long last, after decades of rejectionist attitude, after several cycles of bloodshed and rage, the Palestinians will compromise for only a section of what the Israeli's were ready to recognize as Palestine, back in 1947.

Israel, for its part, is now going back to what for decades used to be the mainstream Zionist attitude: it is once again willing to make an ethical, realistic compromise based on the recognition of the Palestinian's right to a homeland. Recognition for recognition, security for security, good neighborliness for good neighborliness.

And what if they cheat? And what if they take whatever we give them and demand even more, still exercising violence and terror? Within the present proposed settlement, Israel will still be in a position to close in on Palestine and to undo the deal. If the worst comes to the worst, if it turns out that the Peace is no peace, it will always be militarily easier for Israel to break the backbone of a tiny, demilitarized Palestinian entity than to go on and on breaking the backbones of eight-year-old stone-throwing Palestinian kids. The Israeli doves, more than other Israelis, must assume, once peace comes, a clear cut hawkish attitude concerning the duty of the future Palestinian regime to live precisely by the letter and the spirit of its own obligations.

The plan which is now being negotiated, Gaza and Jericho first, is a sober and reasonable option: if the Palestinians want to hold on to Gaza and Jericho, eventually assuming power in other parts of the Occupied Territories, they will have to prove to us and to the whole world, that they have indeed abandoned the ways of violence and terror, that they are capable of suppressing their own fanatics, that they are renouncing the destructive Palestinian Charter and withdrawing from what they used to call 'the right of return'. They will also have to show that they are willing to tolerate in their midst a minority of Israelis who may choose to live where there will be no Israeli government. Israel, for its part, will have genuinely to deliver the initial Zionist promise: to become a source of blessing to its neighbors: to help herself and them in breaking the vicious circle of suffering, despair and poverty, and to embark upon the road to prosperity.

Arafat and Rabin, Peres and Faisal Husseini will be hearing in the near future from some of their compatriots the word 'traitors'- may they wear this title as a decoration for their vision and courage. Churchill, de Gaulle, Ben-Gurion and Sadat also belonged to this honorable 'club of traitors'.

For many years, thinkers of the doveish left in Israel preached an Israeli/Palestinian compromise, roughly similar to the present one. Initially, they only evoked hatred and loathing from all sides. Celebrating our belated triumph, we Israeli doves must bear in mind how painful these days are for the believers in a 'greater Israel'. Even in the present storm of heated controversy, we must remember that the Israeli opponents are not just the warmongers. Most of them are Israelis who are genuinely afraid that the sky is about to fall in on them, and that their homes and their country are in mortal danger. We have to treat their feelings with understanding and respect, as long as these feelings are manifested in lawful ways. It is crucial that we make every effort to ensure that peace is not

Masterpeace
Ophir Paz-Israeli
1988

As Director of Escola, a college of
design in Tel Aviv, the artist organized a poster exhibition to celebrate Israel's 40th anniversary of
independence. This poster was his
entry. A simple request for what
often seems to be unobtainable.

built upon anyone's loss and humiliation. It is crucial that we struggle for the right of those Israelis who would prefer to go on living faithfully, in peace and safety, in the regions under future Palestinian administration. We may even hope that, in the future, these Israelis will become a bridge of good neighborliness- and will become so with the same enthusiasm and devotion with which they have tried so far to serve as a bridgehead for extended frontiers.

The labor of peacemaking is no matter of emotional outbursts. There is no chance of simply jumping from a twenty-year-old blood feud into a friendship. The labor of peacemaking calls for vision and calculation, for wisdom and generosity and caution, for remembering the malignant past without becoming its slaves. For so many years, we Israelis have told ourselves, sometimes rightly, sometimes as a result of a spasm of fear and suspicion, that we have no partner to talk to, that there is no point in playing chess with ourselves: that we shouldn't place the cart before the horse, that we'll cross the bridge when we get to it.

Well then: we have come to the bridge.

To be more precise, we have reached the point where we and they must begin building the bridge.

Had Israel stuck to the slogan of a 'greater Israel', had Israel continued oppressing and humiliating the Palestinians, trying to turn them into submissive slaves within our expanded borders, their radicalization would have increased to a point where they- and other Arab nations- might have become united under the green flag of despair, waved by ecstatic fundamentalist Islam. Had the Palestinians continued to insist on getting everything or nothing they might have brought upon themselves, upon us, upon the entire region, the horror of a doomsday destruction.

And now, in the shadow of these dangers, it looks as if we and they are about to achieve a viable compromise.

From a Zionist perspective, it may be that in the future people may regard the year 1993 as the end of our one hundred years of solitude in the Land of Israel. This may be the end of the prologue for Zionism, and now, perhaps, it's time to begin the Israeli story proper, to consolidate Israel as a safe, legitimate home for the Jewish people and its Arab citizens; a focus of creative energies; a source of blessing for Israel's neighbors- including the Palestinian neighbors.

There are no sweet compromises. Every compromise entails renouncing certain dreams and longings, limiting some appetites, giving up the fulfillment of certain aspirations, but only a fanatic finds compromise more bitter than death. This is why uncompromising fanaticism always and everywhere exudes the stench of death. Whereas compromise is in the essence of life itself.

The Torah says: 'Thou shalt opt for life.'

Let us opt for life.

(translation by Ora Cummings)

Yes to Peace
Rami and Jacky-Israel

The image suggests the obvious reason for peace.

כן לשלום!

Glenn Frankel

Two Hearts

Glenn Frankel was Jerusalem
bureau chief for the Washington
Post and winner of the 1989
Pulitzer Prize for Internationl
Reporting for his coverage of the
intifada. His book, *Beyond the
Promised Land: Jews and Arabs on
the Hard Road to a New Israel,* won
the National Jewish Book Award.

Wrapped inside their own intimate political dramas, Palestinians and Israelis usually viewed each other as the impersonal symbol on the other side of the wall. Israelis saw the masked, blood-crazed Arab stone thrower, Palestinians the armed and arrogant Israeli soldier or the gun-toting, Bible-quoting, fanatical settler. Each impinged on the other's lives only as an aggressor and an agent of disaster. Rarely did the human being behind the image break through—and even then, the result often only added further to the pain.

Mohammed Nasir Hawwash was a child of the Nablus casbah. He had been born and raised in its alleyways, one of eight children brought up in a run-down, cold water flat in a makeshift tenement building beside a winding hillside road. He was 20 years old in December of 1988 and he worked as a sewing machine operator in a local clothing factory. By custom he would have remained in his father's house until he married and perhaps, if the money was not sufficient, for a long time after that. He was, his father later recalled, a dependable son who faithfully brought home his paycheck and honored his parents. Had he the choice, the family insisted, Nasir would never have placed his father in the terrible position of having to decide the fate of another man.

It was the end of the first year of the intifada and Nablus was a kingdom of disorder governed by the young militants. Israeli soldiers entered the claustrophobic confines of the casbah as if they were invading enemy territory. On one particularly brutal day soldiers shot dead a 14-year-old boy. Two days later, on an ash-gray Friday morning, the new martyr was to be buried. Caches of stones and bottles had been stacked along the route of the funeral procession. Trouble was more than expected; it was inevitable.

There is no reliable way to reconstruct exactly what happened that morning. The official Israeli account said that soldiers opened fire when their lives were endangered by rioters throwing stones. The unofficial Palestinian version asserts that the soldiers provoked the violence by positioning themselves along the procession's route and daring the youths to attack them. Nasir Hawwash was among the youths. Whether he was a ringleader or a stone thrower or an innocent bystander is not clear. Israeli sharpshooters shot eight young Palestinians in the head. Five died immediately, but three others lay in coma, brain-dead but still alive. They were taken to Makassed Hospital in East Jerusalem with bullets in their brains. Nasir was among them.

Two days later, an Israeli businessman named Yehiel Yisrael was wheeled into an operating room at Hadassah Hospital across town for open heart surgery. He was 46, a husband and a father of three. His family lived in a large apartment in the quiet, prosperous, tree-lined Beit Hakerem neighborhood—a long long way from Nablus. The operation should have been a routine valve replacement procedure but something went badly wrong and Yisrael was soon near death. He needed another heart and he needed it quickly. Later that

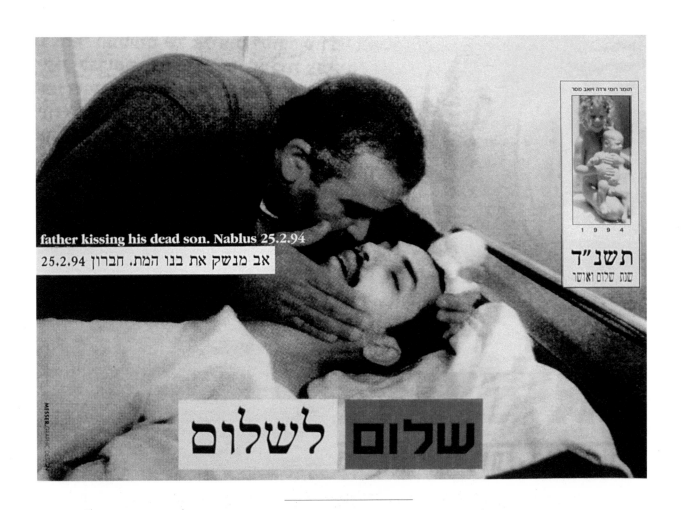

Goodbye to Peace
Varda Messer-Israeli
1994

The Israeli artist juxtaposes a
photograph of her children over
the image of an Arab father kiss-
ing his dead son goodbye to
bring the message home.

No Lifeguard (Saviour) on Duty
Joseph Jibri-Israeli
1991

Jibri uses a photograph of a lifeguard tower on the beaches of
Tel Aviv. In Hebrew, the words
'lifeguard' and 'saviour' are the
same, indicating the mood of
the Israeli people— tired of the
lack of progress in the peace
process.

day a relative watching Israel Television's nightly news broadcast saw the scene from Makassed, the three young men in coma, the grieving families. Here perhaps was Yehiel Yisrael's chance to live.

The Yisraels' surgeon phoned Makassed and determined that of the three dying men, only Nasir Hawwash's heart was suitable for transplant. But the hospital could not approve the procedure without his family's permission. The Yisraels did not approach the Hawwashes themselves, but a family friend who spoke broken Arabic placed a call to Makassed. She reached Mohammed's older brother Ghassan, 27, who was appalled that an Israeli could ask such a thing. She told him, "This is how we'll make peace between Arabs and Jews." He was not buying. "How can you make peace when you shoot someone and then take the heart to give life to another Israeli?" he asked her.

Yehiel Yisrael's wife, Yehudit, pleaded. "We are all people and if we cannot help each other, then we have no values, we have no basis to live on."

The Yisrael family enlisted the help of Jerusalem Mayor Teddy Kollek and a handful of left-wing members of the Israeli Knesset, and there was talk of a large cash payment to the Hawwashes—more money than they would have seen in a lifetime. Palestinian figures became involved, including several who were prominent supporters of the PLO. The sessions between the two sides began to take on the air of a Middle East peace conference. People argued, they made speeches; there was much talk, a lot of anger, but little communication.

Arab sentiment divided three ways. Those associated with Fatah, the main PLO wing, encouraged the family to donate the heart as a gesture of humanitarianism that might send a positive message to Israelis and shame them as well. There were Islamic fundamentalists who opposed the donation for religious reasons. And there were radicals who warned, as one later put it, "If we give the Israelis this heart, soon they'll be shooting us for our organs."

In the end, Nasir's father Jammal said no. Within a few days, Yehiel Yisrael was dead. "Politics won and life lost," said Dedi Zucker, one of the Israeli lawmakers who had sought to arrange the transplant despite strong opposition from his own wife, who said it was too much to ask from a bereaved Palestinian family. Rumor on the West Bank said the father had bowed to the pressure from fundamentalists, but Jammal Hawwash did not characterize it that way. A few weeks later, the pain of his decision still sat visibly on his tired shoulders and he slumped despondently in a dank brown armchair in his small flat. The mourning period was far from over and blurry color Polaroids of Nasir's smiling, chunky face lined the walls. He had not wanted anyone to die, Jammal Hawwash said, not his own son, not the Israeli. But he could not cope with having his son's heart removed, even after death, to go to someone whose fellow tribesmen had killed him. He was angry, he was miserable and he was bewildered all at the same time. He did not know why God had singled him out for such a terrible test. Worse, he could not say if he had passed or failed.

"What did they want from me?" he asked. "This was my son. They took him away, then they wanted his body. This I could not give."

Adapted from *Beyond the Promised Land: Jews and Arabs on the Hard Road to a New Israel* (New York: Simon & Schuster, 1994).

48

Yehuda Amichai

Half the People of the World

Half the people in the world
love the other half,
half the people
hate the other half.
Must I because of this half and that half
go wandering and changing ceaselessly
like rain in its cycle,
must I sleep among rocks,
and grow rugged like the trunks of olive trees,
and hear the moon barking at me,
and camouflage my love with worries,
and sprout like frightened grass between the railroad tracks,
and live underground like a mole,
and remain with roots and not with branches,
and not feel my cheek against the cheek of angels,
and love in the first cave,
and marry my wife beneath a canopy
of beams that support the earth,
and act out my death, always
till the last breath and the last
words and without ever understanding,
and put flagpoles on top of my house
and a bomb shelter underneath. And go out on roads
made only for returning and go through
all the appalling stations-
cat, stick, fire, water, butcher,
between the kid and the angel of death?

Yehuda Amichai, a poet who lives
in Jerusalem, has published many
books of poetry, novels and plays
which have been translated into 20
languages. He does not want to be
connected to any concrete style or
literary direction. In his poems,
he mixes Old Jewish, Asian and
German traditions.

Stop It!
Asher Kalderon-Israeli

With images of war, the artist
says 'Stop!'

Ghassan Kanafani

Umm Saad (an extract from the novel)

Ghassan Kanafani, creator and editor of the Al-hadaf, a weekly started in 1969 for the Popular Front for the Liberation of Palestine (PFLP), is regarded as one of the most influential Palestinian writers of prose. His works are dedicated to the Palestinian cause, but have universal appeal. They include five novels, two of them unfinished, five collections of short stories (including *Men in the Sun*), two plays and two studies of Palestinian literature. Kanafani was killed, along with his neice, in 1972 in a car bomb.

untitled
Abd El Rahman Al Muzzayin-
Palestinian

The symbols of the Palestinian people are all evident in this painting turned into a poster produced by the PLO—the woman as mother Palestine in traditional embroidered dress, the Dome of the Rock and the doves of peace.

Umm Saad lived for countless years with my family in al-Ghabasiya, and since then she has lived for a crushing load of years in the torment of the camps. She still comes to our house every Tuesday. She looks at things, conscious of her part in them to the marrow of her bones, and she looks on me as a son, pouring into my ear the tales of her misery, her joy, and her troubles. But never once does she complain.

She is a woman of about forty, I think, with a strength greater than rock and a patience more than endurance itself. She spends every day of her week coming and going, living her life ten times over in toil to snatch for herself and her children an honest bite to eat.

I have known her for years. She represents something in my life which I cannot do without. When she knocks on the door and puts her poor belongings down in the hall, I am enveloped in the smell of the camps, in their misery and deep-rooted steadfastness, their poverty and hopes. Again my mouth is filled with the bitterness which I have tasted year after year until it has sickened me.

Last Tuesday she came as usual, put down her poor bundle, and turned to face me.
'Cousin, I want to tell you something. Saad has gone.'
'Where?'
'To them.'
'Who?'
'The fadayeen.'
A cautious silence fell between us, and suddenly I saw her sitting there, ageing, strong, her life worn away by the wretched toil. Her hands were folded on her lap, and I could see the palms, dry as blocks of wood, cracked like an old tree-trunk. Through the furrows which years of hard work had traced in them I could see her sorry journey with Saad, from the time when he was a child until he grew to maturity. Those firm hands had nourished him as the earth nourishes the stem of a tender plant, and now they had opened suddenly, and the bird which had nestled there for twenty years had flown away.
'He's joined the fedayeen.'
I was still gazing at her hands, folded palms upwards like two disappointed creatures, crying out from the heart, chasing the man who was leaving everything for danger and the unknown. Why, O God, must mothers lose their sons? For the first time I was seeing that heartbreaking situation, at a word's distance from me, as though we were in a Greek theater living out a scene of inconsolable grief. Trying to distract her and myself, I asked her:
'What did he tell you?'
'He didn't say anything. He simply went. In the morning his friend told me he had gone to join them.'
'Didn't he tell you before that he would go?'
'Oh yes. And I believed him. I know Saad, and I knew that he would go.'
'Then why were you surprised?'

كلّنا فدائيّون

'Me? I wasn't surprised. I'm just telling you about it. I said to myself: "You may be interested to know what's become of Saad." '

The hands, folded in her lap, moved, and I could see them, beautiful, strong, always capable of making something. I doubted whether they were really lamenting. She added:

'No, I said to my neighbor this morning: "I wish I had ten like him." I'm tired, cousin. I've worn my life threadbare in that camp. Every morning I say "O, Lord." Twenty years have passed now, and if Saad doesn't go, who will?' She stood up, and an air of simplicity came over the room, Everything seemed more familiar, and I could see the houses of al-Ghabasiya in it again. But I followed her to the kitchen. There she laughed as she looked at me, saying:

'I told the woman sitting beside me on the bus that my son had become a combatant... I told her that I loved him and missed him, but he was a true son of his mother. Do you think they'll give him a machine gun?'

'They always give their men machine guns.'

'And what about food?'

'They have enough to eat, and they're given cigarettes.'

'Saad doesn't smoke, but I'm sure that he will learn to there. Light of his mother's eyes! I wish he were nearby, so I could take him food every day which I had cooked myself.'

'He'll eat the same as his companions.'

'God bless them all.' She fell silent for a moment, then turned to face me. 'Do you think he'd be pleased if I went to see him? I can save the money for the journey, and get there in two days.' She remembered something and finished off: 'Do you know something? Children are slavery. If I didn't have these two children I'd have followed him. I'd have lived there with him. In a tent, yes, a tent in a refugee camp is quite different from one in a guerilla base. I would have lived with him, cooked for them, done all I could for them. But children are slavery.'

I replied:

'There's no need to visit him there. Let him manage alone. A man who joins the fedayeen doesn't need his mother to look after him anymore.'

She wiped her hands on her apron. Deep in her eyes I glimpsed something like disappointment, that terrifying moment when a mother feels that she can be dispensed with and thrown into a corner like an object worn out with use. She came closer, asking:

'Do you really think so? Do you think there's no point in my going to the commander there and asking him to keep an eye on him?' She hesitated, feeling torn in two. Then she asked:

'Or could you ask his commander to keep an eye on him? Say to him: "look after Saad, may God give your children long life."'

'How?' I replied. 'You can't ask someone to look after a guerilla.'

'Why?'

'Because you'd be asking his commander to arrange things so that he stayed out of danger. But Saad himself, and his companions, believe the best way to look after them would be to send them to war immediately.'

Again she sat there, but she seemed stonger than I had ever seen her. I watched a mother's perplexity and torment in her eyes and hard hands. At last she had made up her mind. 'I tell you what. When you tell his commander to look after him, advise him not to annoy him. Say to him: "Umm Saad begs you, for your mother's sake, to let Saad do what he wants. He's a good lad, and when he wants something and it doesn't happen he gets very miserable." Tell him, I beg you, to let Saad do what he wants. If he wants to go to war, then why doesn't his commander send him?'

אברהם גדליה והוגט אלחדד-עזרן מציגים:

עוונת הדובדבנים

סרטו של חיים בוזגלו

■ משתתפים: גיל פרנק, עידית טפרסון, ששון גבאי, צחי נוי, דוויד מילטון ג'ונס, אבי גילאור, אל יצפאן ■ צילום: אורן שמוקלר ■ עריכה: ערה לפיד
■ מוסיקה: עדי רנרט ■ קולות: אתי אנקרי ■ במאי: חיים בוזגלו ■ תסריט: חיים בוזגלו בשיתוף עם הירש גודמן ■ מפיק בפועל: ריקי שלח
■ הסרט הופק בהשתתפות: הקרן לעידוד קולנוע ישראלי-איכותי, משרד החינוך והתרבות, משרד התעשייה והמסחר ■

Sara Lemel

The Next War

2cd

Every time a baby boy is born in Israel
his mother says: This one will not have to
go to the army.
There will be peace by then.
But as he grows up she slowly realizes
that nothing has changed.
He has to go like all the others had to
and there is nothing she can do about it.
This sad ritual repeats itself every generation
and almost half a century has passed already
since the establishment of the State of Israel.

But now everything is different.
Before the start of the peace process,
there always had been the feeling that
there was no other choice but to fight.
But now we had another choice and I am afraid
we are letting it pass away.
When my baby boy will be 18 years old,
I will just not let them take him to war.
They can play their bloody games
without him.

Sara Lemel is a correspondent for the German Press Agency (dpa) in Tel Aviv. She received her Master's Degree in Strategic Studies from Tel Aviv University and is married to Yossi Lemel. They have one son.

The Cherry Season
Yossi Lemel-Israeli

A movie poster for a cynical film about a group of soldiers serving in the Lebanon War.

International Labour Day
Abd El Rahman Al Muzzayin-
Palestinian
1979

The woman symbolizing Palestine wears a traditional dress
and holds in her arms the work-
ers who will someday reclaim
their land. At each end are
peace symbols—the dove and
olive branch, and her head is
crowned with the Dome of the
Rock. The text at bottom is cred-
ited to Abu Amar-Yasir Arafat,
then PLO leader.

(opposite page)

In Memory of the Revolution
artist unknown-Palestinian
1981

The central figure wears the
traditional kaffiyah head scarf.
Repetition creates a pattern
reminiscent of colorful Arabic
mosaics. The weapon and dove
signify a fight for peace. The
poster was produced by the
PLO faction FATEH.

untitled (2)
Abd El Rahman Al Muzzayin-
Palestinian

Two paintings by Al Muzzayin
recreated as posters for the PLO-
the Palestinian Liberation Organization.

THE REVOLUTION IS PROTECTED
BY IT'S ARMED MASSES

الثورة تحميها جماهيرها المسلحة

**The Revolution is Protected by
its Armed Masses
Abd El Rahman Al Muzzayin-
Palestinian**
(From the collection of Roots
Palestinian Youth Organization,
Washington D.C.)

A painting by Al Muzzayin was
recreated as a poster for the
PLO- the Palestinian Liberation
Organization.

**Fateh-17th Anniversary of the
Revolution
artist unknown-Palestinian**
(From the collection of Roots
Palestinian Youth Organization,
Washington D.C.)

The poster was produced by the
Fateh faction of the PLO.

ثورة ع الاعادي

الذكرى ١٦ لانطلاقة الثورة

David Grossman

A Man is Like a Stalk of Wheat

David Grossman has written children's books, theatre plays and novels which have won him many awards including the Jerusalem Writers Prize and the Prime Minister's Prize for Hebrew Literature. His novels deal with the relations between Israelis and Arabs; *The Yellow Wind* won him international recognition.

Where is Palestine?
Adnan Zubaidy-Palestinian
1993

The artist depicts a youth spraying the words, 'Where is Palestine?' over the sky of Jerusalem. Illegal and punishable by imprisonment, Palestinians still resorted to spray-painting political messages on the walls of the city. Printing presses were illegal in the Occupied Territories, as was the production of anti-Israeli material, so the walls became their means for disseminating information and political propaganda. Some youths were shot and killed while writing graffiti on walls.

On a day of turbid rain, at the end of March, I turn off the main road leading from my house in Jerusalem to Hebron, and enter the Deheisha refugee camp. Twelve thousand Palestinians live here in one of the highest population densities in the world; the houses are piled together, and the house of every extended family branches out in ugly cement growths, rooms and niches, rusty iron beams spread throughout as sinews, jutting like disconnected fingers.

In Deheisha, drinking water comes from wells. The only running water is the rainwater and sewage flowing down the paths between the houses. I soon give up picking my way between the puddles; there is something ridiculous—almost unfair—about preserving such refinement here, in the face of a few drops of filth.

Beside each house—a yard. They are small, fenced in with corrugated aluminum, and very clean. A large jar filled with springwater and covered with cloth stands in each yard. But every person here will tell you without hesitation that the water from the spring of his home village was sweeter. "In Ain Azrab"—she sighs (her name is Hadija, and she is very old)—our water was so clear and healthy that a dying man once immersed himself, drank a few mouthfuls, and washed—and was healed on the spot." She cocks her head, drills me with an examining gaze, and mocks: "So, what do you think of that?"

I discover—with some bafflement, I admit—that she reminds me of my grandmother and her stories about Poland, from which she was expelled. About the river, about the fruit there. Time has marked both their faces with the same lines, of wisdom and irony, of great skepticism toward all people, both relatives and strangers.

"We had a field there. A vineyard. Now see what a flowering garden we have here," and she waves her brown, wrinkled hand over the tiny yard.

"But we made a garden," murmurs her daughter-in-law, a woman of wild, gypsy, unquiet beauty. "We made a garden in tin cans." She nods toward the top of the cinder-block fence, where several pickle cans bring forth red geraniums, in odd abundance, as if drawing their life from a far source of fruitfulness, of creation.

A strange life. Double and split. Everyone I spoke to in the camp is trained—almost from birth—to live this double life: they sit here, very much here, because deprivation imposes sobriety with cruel force, but they are also there. That is—among us. In the villages, in the cities. I ask a five-year-old boy where he is from, and he immediately answers, "Jaffa," which is today part of Tel Aviv. "Have you ever seen Jaffa?" "No, but my grandfather saw it." His father, apparently, was born here, but his grandfather came from Jaffa. "And is it beautiful, Jaffa?" "Yes. It has orchards and vineyards and the sea."

And farther down, where the path slopes, I meet a young girl sitting on a cement wall, reading an illustrated magazine. Where are you from? She is from Lod, not far from the Ben-Gurion International Airport, forty years ago an Arab town. She is sixteen. She tells me, giggling, of the beauty of Lod. Of its houses, which were big as palaces. "And in every room a hand-painted carpet. And the land was wonderful and the sky was always blue."

I remembered the wistful lines of Yehuda Halevy, "The taste of your sand—more pleasant to my mouth than honey," and Bialik, who sang to the land which "the spring eternally adorns," how wonderfully separation beautifies the beloved, and how strange it is, in the barrenness of the gray cement of Deheisha, to hear sentences so full of lyric beauty, words spoken in a language more exalted than the everyday, poetic but of established routine, like a prayer or an oath: "And the tomatoes there were red and big, and everything came to us from the earth, and the earth gave us and gave us more."

"Have you visited there, Lod?" "Of course not." "Aren't you curious to see it now?" "Only when we return."

This is how the others answer me also. The Palestinians, as is well known, are making use of the ancient Jewish strategy of exile and have removed themselves from history. They close their eyes against harsh reality, and stubbornly clamping down their eyelids, they fabricate their Promised Land. "Next year in Jerusalem," said the Jews in Latvia and in Krakow and in San'a, and the meaning was that they were not willing to compromise. Because they had no hope for any real change. He who has nothing to lose can demand everything; and until his Jerusalem becomes real, he will do nothing to bring it closer. And here also, again and again, that absolute demand: everything. Nablus and Hebron and Jaffa and Jerusalem. And in the meantime—nothing. In the meantime, abandoned physically and spiritually. In the meantime, a dream and a void.

22nd Year on the Road to Victory
Habib Jasa'a-Palestinian
1986

Produced outside the Occupied Territories, this poster includes two doves of peace created from the Palestinian flag. The Jaffa orange is in the background with a map of Palestine.

فلسطين

١٥ أيّار

جمعية الهلال C الأحمر الفلسطيني

جهاز الإعلام والتثقيف المركزي

David Grossman

The Yellow Wind

On the slope of the hill in Deheisha, I passed a group of small children racing upward. Rowda. An Arab kindergarten. Two teachers (Don't give our names, but you can quote) and thirty-five children from two to five years old. The Deheisha kindergarten.

I want to expand a little on this subject: the small children, nameless, with running noses, the ones we see along the roads, playing by the passing cars. These are the children who in '67 sold us figs for a grush and washed our parents' cars for ten grush. And afterwards they grew up a little and became the shebab, you know, the ones with the look of hate in their eyes, rioting in the streets and throwing stones at our soldiers, tying a lasso to the crown of a cypress tree, bending it to the ground, attaching a Palestinain flag to it, and freeing the tree—and you, the soldier, go cut down the moon; and afterwards they grew a little more, and from among them came the ones who make the Molotov cocktails and the bombs. They are the same children from '67. Nothing has changed in the refugee camps, and their future is etched on their faces like an ancient, fossilized record.

For now, they are little children in a kindergarten. One group shouts and cheers, and after making a conscious effort—necessary, perhaps, for all strangers and for Jews and Israelis in particular—I begin to differentiate their faces, their voices, their smiles, their characters, and slowly also their beauty and delicacy, and this is not easy. It requires an investment of energy on my part, since I also have trained myself to look at Arabs with that same blurred vision which makes it easier for me (only me?) to deal with their chiding, accusing, threatening presence, and during this month of encounters with them I must do exactly the opposite, enter the vortex of my greatest fear and repulsion, direct my gaze at the invisible Arab, face this forgotten reality, and see how—as in the process of developing a picture—it emerges before me slowly, slowly from the emulsion in the darkroom of my fears and my sublimations.

**As the Wound gets Larger-
Patriotism and the Country
get Closer
artist unknown-Palestinian**
(from the collection of Roots
Palestinian Youth Organization,
Washington D.C.)

The poster was produced by the
Palestinian Organization of the
Red Crescent (same as the Red
Cross)

untitled
Zeev Harrari-Israeli
1988

The poster produced for the 40th anniversary of Israel shows a patch work of Jewish and Arab 'settlements'—patches symbolizing the sewn Star of David worn by Jews during Nazi occupation; the Arab patchs are made from the kaffiyah. The militaristic colors on a dark background are an antithesis of the blue and white Israeli national colors.

(Opposite page)

And the Wolf will dwell with the Lamb
Gad Ulman-Israeli
1990

Produced on the occasion of the 3000th year of Jerusalem, this poster is a commentary on the relationship between the Jews and the Arabs.

ירושלים 3000 שנה
القدس. ثلاثة آلاف سنة

Jerusalem. three thousand years

AND THE WOLF WILL DWELL WITH THE LAMB...   ...וגר זאב עם כבש
وسكن الذئب مع الكبش

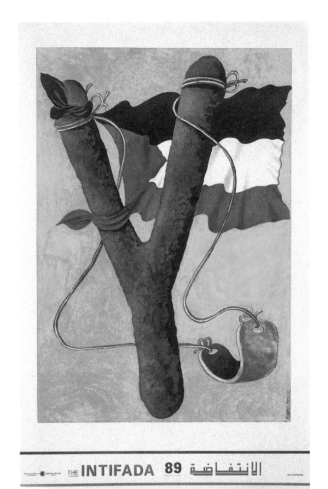

Intifada 89
artist unknown
(from the collection of the Middle
East Division of the Harvard College
Library)

The slingshot was used by
demonstrating youth during the
intifada for lack of any other
weapons. A Palestinian flag rip-
ples in the background. These
posters produced by the PLO
were printed outside the Occupied Territories and disseminat-
ed around the world to encour-
age support. The artists were
frequently exiled Palestinian
artists or other nationalities
who contributed their talents.

Intifada 89
artist unknown
(from the collection of the Middle
East Division of the Harvard College
Library)

Arafat, then the PLO leader,
stands with a crying child
behind barbed wire, which
symbolically and literally kept
Palestinians from their homeland.

Palestine-Intifada 89
artist unknown
(from the collection of the Middle East Division of the Harvard College Library)

The Dove of Peace sits on a roadside signpost. The post is painted in the colors of the Palestinian flag.

Land Day
artist unknown
(from the collection of the Middle East Division of the Harvard College Library)

The tree is made up of the colors and shape of the Palestinian flag.

(opposite page)   (opposite page)

Prisoner's Day (Hope)
Sliman Mansour-Palestinian

A painting was made into a
poster to remind us of the
Palestinian prisoners in Israeli
camps at the time. The message
is hopeful with the rainbow
inside the prison made of the
colors of the Palestinian flag
(red, black, green and white)
turning into the colors of the
rainbow outside the prison bars.

The Road to Victory
Taleb Dweik-Palestinian

The long winding road to victory
is made from the long sinuous
neck of the peace dove. A black
Star of David looms subtly yet
ominously in the background.

untitled
Nabil Anani-Palestinian

The artist depicts the bound
hands of the prisoner in front of
a yellow crescent.

Yoram Binur

My Enemy, My Self

There was one night at Hatuki that brought home most strongly all the feelings of frustration and humiliation that I had experienced as an Arab worker. Ofra's sister, Michal, had a boyfriend, a handsome man with an athletic build, who used to come to the pub during work hours in order to help out or just to sit over a drink in his girlfriend's company.

It was about two in the morning and most of the customers were gone. I was in the kitchen washing dishes and returning leftovers to the refrigerator so they could be recycled the following day, when Michal and her boyfriend, laughing excitedly, pushed their way into the kitchen—which hardly had enough room for one man alone to move around in. They squeezed themselves into a small corner between me and the refrigerator and proceeded to kiss each other passionately.

I lowered my eyes and concentrated on washing the dirty dishes in the sink, carefully going over each plate, so I wouldn't embarrass them with my presence. The breathing got heavier as they got bolder, and for a fleeting moment I thought I might as well enjoy the little scene that had come my way. I ventured a peek at them out of the corner of my eye.

Then a sort of trembling suddenly came over me. I realized that they had not meant to put on a peep show for my enjoyment. Those two were not the least bit concerned with what I saw or felt even when they were practically fucking under my nose. For them, I simply didn't exist. I was invisible, a nonentity! It's difficult to describe the feeling of deep humiliation which I experienced. Looking back, I think it was the most degrading moment I had during my entire posing adventure.

Yorum Binur, an Israeli correspondent for Arab Affairs in the West Bank and Gaza, has written for the weekly Kol Ha'ir (The Voice of the City) in Jerusalem since 1984. In 1989 he posed as a Palestinian in a variety of situations within Israeli society, and recorded his feelings as well as the reactions of those involved. This story takes place at the Hataki pub, its name meaning parrot, and its owner named Ofra. Binur, under the guise of Ali was hired as kitchen help.

Bunker
Asher Arnon-Israeli

A poster for a movie about young Israeli soldiers and their 'love affair' with their power and weapons and the pressures of military service.

يــوم الـطـفـل الـفـلـطـيـنـي ٧/١٥
يـخـصـص ريـعـه لـتطـويـر ريـاض اطـفـال غـسـان كـنفاني

Yehuda Amichai

The Place Where
We are Right

From the place where we are right

flowers will never grow

in the spring

The place where we are right

is hard and trampled

like a yard

But doubts and loves

dig up the world

like a mole, a plow

And a whisper will be heard in the place

where the ruined

house once stood

Year of the Child
Adnan Zubaidy-Palestinian

The artist shows a child in a typical embroidered dress engaged in a child's activity of picking flowers. Behind her looms the bulldozer used for the systematic demolition of Palestinian homes and villages by the Israeli government.

Yorum Binur

Second Thoughts

About a year before I began my posing project a friend approached me with a bundle of tattered photographs that were yellowing with age. "I found them in a garbage can on Harakevet Street in Bak'a. There are alot of other papers there. Maybe you'll find them interesting?" Bak'a is a neighborhood in Jerusalem that had been built and populated by wealthy Arab families. After 1948 the buildings were occupied by Jews. I went over there immediately. The garbage can that my friend described was brimming with old papers and files, in English and in Arabic, and a few dozen family photographs. Some of the papers had been blown by the wind along the railroad tracks that ran parallel to the street. I crammed everything I could get my hands on into the sidecar of my motorbike. My dog, Katanchik, sat on top of the pile and his weight was sufficient to keep it from all blowing away.

When I sifted through the material at home I realized that I had the entire history of a well-to-do Arab family spread out before me. The Jewish tenants of the house had apparently been cleaning out the storeroom and the old records of the Farah family, onetime owners of the house, were thrown out. A brief inquiry on the phone, with the aid of the staff of AL Fajr, revealed that one member of the family, a man responsible for agricultural development projects in the West Bank, lived in East Jerusalem. I brought the papers to his house and with great excitement we went over the old photographs of his family, friends, and in-laws.

Design & Society
David Tartakover-Israeli
1991

While international designers were attending a conference in Israel titled 'Design & Society,' Palestinians' homes were being demolished or sealed with concrete blocks by the Israeli government.

Ghassan Kanafani

A Letter to His Son

I heard you in the other room asking your mother: "Mama, am I a Palestinian?" When she answered : "Yes," a heavy silence fell on the whole house. It was as if something hanging over our heads had fallen, its noise exploding, then—silence.

Afterwards...I heard you crying. I could not move. There was something bigger than my awareness being born in the other room through your bewildered sobbing. It was as if a blessed scalpel was cutting up your chest and there the heart that belongs to you... I was unable to move to see what was happening in the other room. I knew, however, that a distant homeland was being born again: hills, plains, olive groves, dead people, torn banners and folded ones, all cutting their way into a future of flesh and blood and being born in the heart of another child... Do not believe that man grows. No; he is born suddenly—a word, in a moment, penetrates his heart to a new throb. One scene can hurl him down from the ceiling of childhood on to the ruggedness of the road.

untitled
Lela Shawa-Palestinian
1992
(from Dana Bartelt's collection)

The young Palestinian boy
standing in front of a wall full
of graffiti is a 'target' for Israeli
soldiers.

Ghassan Kanafani

Letter from Gaza

Dear Mustafa,

I have now received your letter, in which you tell me that you've done everything necessary to enable me to stay with you in Sacramento. I've also received news that I have been
accepted in the department of Civil Engineering in the University of California. I must
thank you for everything, my friend. But it'll strike you as rather odd when I proclaim
this news to you—and make no doubt about it, I feel no hesitation at all, in fact I am
pretty well positive that I have never seen things so clearly as I do now. No, my friend,
I have changed my mind. I won't follow you to 'the land where there is greenery, water
and lovely faces' as you wrote. No, I'll stay here, and I won't ever leave.

I am really upset that our lives won't continue to follow the same course, Mustafa. For I
can almost hear you reminding me of our vow to go on together, and of the way we used
to shout: 'We'll get rich!' But there's nothing I can do, my friend. Yes, I still remember the
day when I stood in the hall of Cairo airport, pressing your hand and staring at the fren-
zied motor. At that moment everything was rotating in time with the ear- splitting motor,
and you stood in front of me, your round face silent.

Your face hadn't changed from the way it used to be when you were growing up in the
Shajiya quarter of Gaza, apart from those slight wrinkles. We grew up together, understanding each other completely, and we promised to go on together till the end. But...

'There's a quarter of an hour left before the plane takes off. Don't look into space like that.
Listen! You'll go to Kuwait next year, and you'll save enough from your salary to uproot
you from Gaza and transplant you to California. We started off together and we must
carry on....'

At that moment I was watching your rapidly moving lips. That was always your manner
of speaking, without commas or full stops. But in an obscure way I felt that you were not
completely happy with your flight. You couldn't give three good reasons for it. I too suffered from this wrench, but the clearest thought was: why don't we abandon this Gaza
and flee?

Why don't we? Your situation had begun to improve, however. The Ministry of Education
in Kuwait had given you a contract though it hadn't given me one. In the trough of misery where I existed you sent me small sums of money. You wanted me to consider them
as loans, because you feared that I would feel slighted. You knew my family circum-
stances in and out; you knew that meager salary in the UNRWA schools was inadequate
to support my mother, my brother's widow and her four children.

'Listen carefully. Write to me every day...every hour...every minute! The plane's just leaving. Farewell! Or rather, till we meet again!

Your cold lips brushed my cheek, you turned your face away from me towards the plane,
and when you looked at me again I could see your tears.

Later the Ministry of Education in Kuwait gave me a contract. There's no need to repeat
to you how my life there went in detail. I always wrote to you about everything. My life
there had a gluey, vacuous quality as though I were a small oyster, lost in oppressive lone-

Pain
David Tartakover-Israeli

The word 'pain' in Hebrew also
means 'as a father' and appeals
to Israeli soldiers, who might
also be fathers of children like
the little Palestinian girl who lost
an eye by an Israeli rubber bullet,
not to serve in the Occupied
Territories. The poster was produced as part of the Yesh Gul
(There is a Limit) Movement.

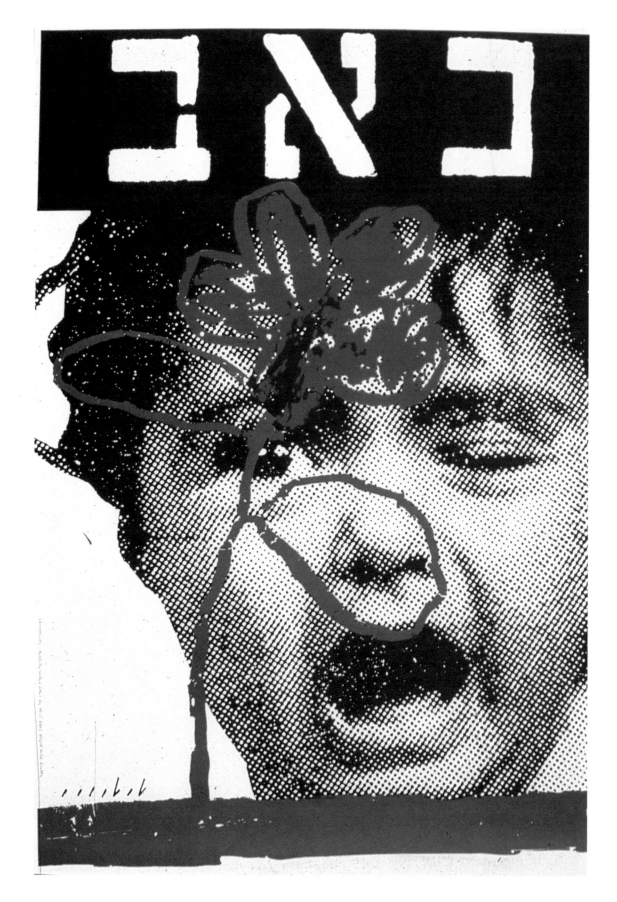

liness, slowly struggling with a future as dark as the beginning of the night, caught in a rotten routine, a spewed-out combat with time. Everything was hot and sticky. There was a slipperiness to my whole life, it was all a hankering for the end of the month.

In the middle of the year, that year, the Jews bombarded the central district of Sabha and attacked Gaza, our Gaza, with bombs and flame-throwers. That event might have made some change in my routine, but there was nothing for me to take much notice of; I was going to leave this Gaza behind me and go to California where I would live for myself, my own self which had suffered so long. I hated Gaza and its inhabitants. Everything in the amputated town reminded me of failed pictures painted in grey by a sick man. Yes, I would send my mother and my brother's widow and her children a meager sum to help them to live, but I would liberate myself from this last tie too, there in green California, far from the reek of defeat which for seven years had filled my nostrils. The sympathy which bound me to my brother's children, their mother and mine would never be enough to justify my tragedy in taking this perpendicular dive. It mustn't drag me any farther down than it already had. I must flee!

You know these feelings, Mustafa, because you've really experienced them. What is this ill-defined tie we had with Gaza which blunted our enthusiasm for flight? Why didn't we analyze the matter in such a way as to give it a clear meaning? Why didn't we leave this defeat with it's wounds behind us and move on to a brighter future which would give us a deeper consolation! Why? We didn't exactly know.

When I went on holiday in June and assembled all my possessions, longing for the sweet departure, the start towards those little things which give life a nice, bright meaning, I found Gaza just as I had known it, closed like the introverted lining of a rusted snail-shell thrown up by the waves on the sticky, sandy shore by the slaughterhouse. This Gaza was more cramped than the mind of a sleeper in the throes of a fearful nightmare, with its narrow streets which had their peculiar smell, the smell of defeat and poverty, its houses with their bulging balconies...this Gaza! But what are the obscure causes that draw a man to his family, his house, his memories, as a spring draws a small flock of mountain goats? I don't know. All I know is that I went to my mother in our house that morning. When I arrived my late brother's wife met me there and asked me, weeping, if I would do as her wounded daughter, Nadia, in Gaza hospital wished and visit her in the evening. Do you know Nadia, my brother's beautiful thirteen-year-old daughter?

That evening I bought a pound of apples and set for the hospital to visit Nadia. I knew that there was something about it that my mother and my sister-in-law were hiding from me, something which their tongues could not utter, something strange which I could not put my finger on. I loved Nadia from habit, the same habit that made me love all that generation which had been so brought up on defeat and displacement that it had come to think that a happy life was a kind of social deviation.

What happened at that moment? I don't know. I entered the white room very calm. Ill children have something of saintliness, and how much more so if the child is ill as a result of cruel, painful wounds. Nadia was lying on her bed, her back propped up on a big pillow over which her hair was spread like a thick pelt. There was a profound silence in her wide eyes and a tear always shining in the depths of her black pupils. Her face was calm and still but eloquent as the face of a tortured prophet might be. Nadia was still a child, but she seemed more than a child, much more, and older than a child, much older.

'Nadia!'

I've no idea whether I was the one who said it, or whether it was someone else behind me. But she raised her eyes to me and I felt them dissolve me like a piece of sugar that had fallen into a hot cup of tea. Together with her slight smile I heard her voice.

'Uncle! Have you just come from Kuwait?'

Her voice broke in her throat, and she raised herself with the help of her hands and stretched out her neck towards me. I patted her back and sat down near her.

'Nadia! I've brought you presents from Kuwait, lots of presents. I'll wait till you can leave your bed, completely well and healed, and you'll come to my house and I'll give them to you. I've brought you the red trousers you wrote and asked me for. Yes, I've brought them.'

It was a lie, born of the tense situation, but as I uttered it I felt that I was speaking the truth for the first time. Nadia trembled as though she had had an electric shock, and lowered her head in a terrible silence. I felt the tears wetting the back of my hand.

'Say something, Nadia! Don't you want the red trousers?'

She lifted her gaze to me and made as if to speak, but then she stopped, gritted her teeth and I heard her voice again, coming from far away.

'Uncle!'

She stretched out her hand, lifted the white coverlet with her fingers and pointed to her leg, amputated from the top of the thigh.

My friend...Never shall I forget Nadia's leg, amputated from the top of the thigh. No! Nor shall I forget the grief which had molded her face and merged into its traits for ever. I went out of the hospital in Gaza that day, my hand clutched in silent derision on the two pounds I had brought with me to give Nadia. The blazing sun filled the streets with the color of blood. And Gaza was brand new, Mustafa! You and I never saw it like this. The stone piled up at the beginning of the Shajiya quarter where we lived had a meaning, and they seemed to have been put there for no other reason but to explain it. This Gaza in which we had lived and with whose good people we had spent seven years of defeat was something new. It seemed to me just a beginning. I don't know why I thought it was just a beginning. I imagined that the main street that I walked along on the way back home was only the beginning of a long, long road leading to Safad. Everything in this Gaza throbbed with sadness which was not confined to weeping. It was a challenge; more than that, it was something like reclamation of the amputated leg!

I went out into the streets of Gaza, streets filled with blinding sunlight. They told me that Nadia had lost her leg when she threw herself on top of her little brothers and sisters to protect them from the bombs and flames that had fastened their claws into the house. Nadia could have saved herself, she could have run away, rescued her leg. But she didn't.

Why?

No, my friend, I won't come to Sacramento, and I've no regrets. No, and nor will I finish what we began together in childhood. This obscure feeling that you had as you left Gaza, this small feeling must grow into a giant deep within you. It must expand, you must seek it in order to find yourself, here among the ugly debris of defeat.

I won't come to you. But you, return to us! Come back. To learn from Nadia's leg, amputated from the top of the thigh, what life is and what existence is worth.

Come back, my friend! We are all waiting for you.

Lynne Reid Banks

The Broken Bridge

Lynne Reid Banks has won international acclaim as a children's novelist. Her classic, *The Indian in the Cupboard,* sold 6 million copies and was made into a major motion picture. In 1963, she emigrated from England to Israel and taught English. She now lives in England and works as a reporter, journalist, playwright and novelist.

**Don't Say You Didn't Know
Rami & Jacky-Israeli
1982**

The names of the Palestinian victims beaten to death by Israeli soldiers are listed on the poster. The text refers to the Holocaust and to those claiming "they didn't know" that it was happening, and a plea from the artists not to ignore what is happening in the Occupied Territories.

They were walking through the heat. Even under the big shade trees that hung over the main paths, it was hellishly hot. Drops of sweat ran off Nat's face and arms, and his old legs trembled.

He'd done three hours' work in the sweltering heat of the milking shed, and he needed a long cold drink, a shower, and his bed, in that order. But Nimrod was his favorite grandchild, despite or even because of all his meshuggassen. He gave the boy's shoulder a little squeeze and said, "out with it."

Nimrod said, "Did he do anything bad when he was in the army?"

Nat's mind, torpid with weariness a second before, leaped to the alert like a startled animal. He dropped his hand. Quickly, quickly, he thought, I must think quickly. He's heard something or guessed something. The truth or a lie? Which? Oh God, if only it weren't so hot!

"Why are you asking this now?"

"So there was something."

"Don't cross-examine me like that son!" he said sharply. "I asked a simple question. Why are you asking?"

"He said something. It could—I mean, it could have been just a...general remark. But—"

"What did he say?" Play for time. Think, man. He's so young. I don't understand it. I can't excuse it. How could a young, innocent kid who's seen nothing of life? It could damage him. Enough damage already! Enough! God, this country! I'm too old for all this!"

"He said," said Nimrod slowly and carefully, as if the words were hurting his mouth but would hurt more if he spoke them, "something about the bloody situation and soldiers like him...beating people up...and breaking—" He stopped. Then he made himself go on. "Breaking their arms."

They had reached the house. Instead of going inside into the blessed coolness he longed for, Nat led Nimrod under the sweltering shade of grapevine he had trained above his patio. They sat sown on garden chairs in silence. There was an overpowering smell of cut grass and flowers and the sound of insects among them, the sweet scents and sounds of the natural world going about its business. Nat needed that at this moment.

"Nimrod," he said shakily. "You know that in 1988, when the intifada really got underway, orders were given from very high up that Arabs who attacked the soldiers with stones were to be punished in that way."

"By having their arms broken?"

Nat swallowed and said loudly, "Yes."

"I thought it meant—I didn't think they ...really did it."

"Well, some did. Some took it literally."

"How did—how did they do it?"

Must I put the pictures in his head—those pictures on television that the world saw? Must I do that?

"I don't know," he lied for the first time.

"You must know, Granddad!" Nimrod shouted suddenly.

"All right, I know! They caught them; they tied them up; they took rocks and clubs; they bashed their arms with them. Its very hard to break a man's arm that way. I'm quite sure that often they didn't, that it was just... heavy bruising. A beating. It was a punishment. A punishment that fitted the crime."

"And Yoni did that?" Nimrod's voice was shaking. "Yoni tied men up and bashed them with rocks and clubs?"

Nat found to his dismay that he was crying, the way he had when Yoni had left that time, three years back, after he had come and told him. He couldn't help himself. His throat was aching, and the tears just came. But Nimrod didn't have the pity for him that Nat had tried, so hard, to have for Yonatan. Nimrod needed to drag it all out of him now, and he was ruthless..

"Granddad, did he? Answer me!"

"Once," Nat said. "After he'd done it, he felt sick and ordered his men to stop, but his platoon jeered at him.

"Later his officer got his unit together and asked who was having problems with the orders. Only Yoni put his hand up. His officer said if he didn't have the stomach to do his duty, he didn't deserve the benefits of security earned by others. He ordered him out on patrol with other men who—who were willing to do it, who did it without feelings. He told me he saw things he wouldn't have believed, beatings that went on and on..." He took out a handkerchief and shakily wiped his eyes and blew his nose.

"It's what I'm always saying Nimrodi. I've been saying it for twenty-five years. It's the cursed Occupation. You can't have a nice, kindly, humane occupation of one people by another. Never, not in history, not in this world. You can't liberate land, as the right-wingers called it when our forces won that miraculous victory in 1967. There were a million people on that 'liberated' land." The people weren't liberated. They were conquered.

"They started it. They tried to conquer us. They've never stopped trying. Someone has to lose."

Nat didn't seem to hear him.

"For a long while they kept pretty quiet, and we told ourselves what benign occupiers we were. We even kidded ourselves we were benefiting them—their standard of living improved; we kindly let them work for us, doing all the dirtiest jobs, of course—but the obvious fact is and was, we're on their backs and they hate us, so in the end, after twenty years, they got sick of it and started the intifada, the uprising.

"And for five years we've been fighting them in their streets, where, in my view, we've no business to be. Now, don't get me wrong. Don't think I don't know what would happen in any other country on earth if mobs of civilians ran at soldiers, cursing and hurling rocks; they'd be mowed down without mercy. But we haven't been so merciful. Hundreds of Palestinians are dead; hundreds more injured, young and old. But in all that time only a handful of our people have been seriously hurt or killed by all their stones. Because whatever they tell you, stones are not as lethal as bullets.

Nimrod sat with his hands squeezed between his knees, which were white as two stones themselves. He was not looking at his grandfather.

"But they'd kill all of us if it was the other way around," he muttered.

"I don't doubt it," said Nat. "We're right to be afraid of them. Their religion

The Olive Leaf/Club of Peace
Abe Rosenfeld- Israeli
1989

In Hebrew, the words 'leaf' and 'club' are similar in pronunciation. The artist makes the statement that instead of the olive leaf of peace, the Israeli government ordered more clubs for beatings by Israeli soldiers of Palestinians, which resulted in thousands of broken bones.

אלת השלום

"... יונה עם אלה של זית ..."

encourages them to die in battle, and they kill each other more than we kill them... they're murdering each other every day. For collaboration, for informing, for feuds, for nothing...Don't ask me to explain it. But the intifada, I understand that. There's always been only one way to win freedom: through fighting. It's the way we won ours."

"So why don't we give it to them? Why don't we just give it to them? The West Bank, Gaza, Golan—why don't we just let them have It?"

"It is fear, O little hunter. It is fear."

"What are you talking about?"

"It is a poem, Nimrodi," he said gently. "I mean, we don't give it back to them because we're afraid to. It's the hardest thing on earth to hand your enemy an advantage."

They sat under the vine for a long time. Nat blew his nose one last time and put his arm around his grandson's shoulders. He felt Nimrod unyielding, as stiff as wood, holding himself tight. Old men can cry, soldiers can cry. But boys of sixteen don't cry.

"Do all the soldiers do it? "Nimrod asked. "Beating people, killing them?"

Nat shrugged. "Most of our soldiers don't know what the hell they're doing in those streets," he said. "They're confused, scared, anyone would be. They're trained for battle, not for street riots. They blunder about, pumped full of adrenaline, doing what they think they're supposed to. That's the worst of it. It makes no sense. We go there, they throw stones, we open fire or chase them and beat them—and for what? For what?" He looked away at the green view of kibbutz gardens;." For what great purpose was my sweet grandson turned into a brute even for five minutes?"

"Will I have to do it?" asked Nimrod very quietly.

Nat turned to him fiercely.

"No," he said. "You won't have to do it. And don't you do it. Don't you dare do it and then come crying to me to make you feel better! I told Yoni I understood, but I didn't. I 'forgave' him, whatever that means, when he asked me to, but I've never been able to feel the same about him. I can't go through it again. Maybe I won't be alive to do it when its your turn!"

Nimrod turned to look at him so suddenly he wrenched his neck, but Nat wasn't looking at him now.

"Shoot and cry, that's what they do—beat and cry. They do it, and then they're sorry, and it makes them feel good to be sorry. But it's not good enough. What's been done, the pain, the hatred, can't be canceled with tears, any more than Glen's death could be canceled if the killer came and begged his mother's pardon. So don't you do it, Nimrod. Don't you ever let anyone make you do it.

Because, if they turn you into that kind of man, what it means to me—what its already begun to mean to me—is that I should have stayed in Canada. That it's all been for nothing. That this wonderful country has a cancer eating it. That's what your generation has to fight and chase away, Nimrod. Not a bunch of hyped-up kids."

(opposite page)

Stop Beating
Fawzy El Emrany-Palestinian

An original painted/collage poster is calling for a stop to the Israeli military's practice of beating and shooting Palestinians, some of who demonstrated and participated in the intifada, others who were innocent bystanders or relatives. The artist shows clippings from newspapers and magazines of youthful victims. The artist's brother was taken from his home and beaten by Israeli soldiers, because a demonstration was held in front of his home, even though he did not participate in this demonstration.

THE **INTIFADA** 89 الإنتفاضة

Daoud Kuttab

A Profile of Stonethrowers

Daoud Kuttab is president of the
Jerusalem Film Institute and is a
freelance journalist.

The high level of political conciousness among young Palestinians in the West Bank and Gaza – currently manifested through their central role in the uprising – is inextricably linked to life under occupation. Like young Palestinians in other parts of the Arab world, Palestinians from the refugee camps will tell you the name of the village they are from, despite the fact that that particular village was destroyed when Israel was established, nearly forty years ago. Palestinian children often learn the names of the PLO leaders before they learn to read and write. They can explain the difference between Zionism and Judaism and are able to make a strong argument against any political solution involving Jordan's King Hussein.

But unlike children in refugee camps elsewhere, children born in refugee camps under occupation drink their mother's milk while their camp is under curfew; they wake up in the middle of the night to the sound of rubber bullets and rumors of a possible settler attack. As they grow up, they quickly learn the political lesson of the occupation. Soldiers, batons, tear gas, rubber bullets, arrests, torture, curfews, closure of camp entrances, administrative detention, and town arrests are all prominent entries in the refugee camps' daily dictionary.

The young Palestinian's vocabulary is not, however, restricted to Israeli oppressive action. Early in life, they also learn the language of resistance. Palestinian nationalist trappings decorate the walls of most Palestinian homes. The often unpainted cement walls in the camps are plastered with photos of Palestinian leaders, often cut out from newspapers and magazines. The photo of PLO Chairman Yasir Arafat or the face of the PFLP's female commando Dalal al-Mughrabi is found most often. Posters of popular Palestinian artists like Sliman Mansour's Jamal al-Mahamil (the porter carrying Jerusalem on his back) is frequently framed and hung in the sitting rooms along with high school matriculation certificates and pictures of family members living abroad. Calendars printed by grassroots women's committees or youth movement are also proudly displayed in the homes of most Palestinian refugees. Such calendars generally contain Palestinian national motifs: the Palestinian flag or its colors, the black and white checkered kaffiyah, or a rough sketch of the map of Palestine.

Intifada 1989
artist unknown-Palestinian
1989
(from the collection of the Middle East Division of the Harvard College Library)

A young fighter of the intifada, is depicted here with a slingshot in hand and a tire burning in the background. This practice was employed during riots and demonstrations in order to create heavy smoke to obscure the Israeli soldiers' view of their actions.

But resistance is not simply a political slogan or a nationalistic calendar. It also includes participation in all-day volunteer programs to build a retaining wall or to pave an alley. Activities of this type are generally sponsored by one of the nationalist committees (aligned with one of the PLO factions). They require a great deal of labor power, and everyone, including children, can help, filling buckets with dirt or passing pails of cement. Patriotic songs are sung and the atmosphere has a way of generating enthusiasm among the young. Weddings may also serve to focus or reinforce nationalist sentiment. In many cases songs that are sung mention particular PLO leaders, thus indicating with which of the factions the couple sympathizes.

In school, demonstrations and stone throwing are part of a tradition. School children are well aware of the most recent political events or national anniversaries. They celebrate by playing hooky en masse, usually after the first period, and by throwing stones at passing Israeli vehicles. To throw a stone is to be 'one of the guys'; to hit an Israeli car is to become a hero; and to be arrested and not confess to having done anything is to be a man.

Stone throwing is normally carried out as part of a large demonstration. Demonstrations may arise in response to a particular Israeli action: arrests, provocations, closing the entrance to a camp, injuring camp residents, and the like. They may also coincide with certain national days. Only on rare occasions is stone throwing an isolated incident. In some cases the stone throwing is carried out by small, well-trained teams. More often it is undertaken by a large group of people, including adults, both men and women, who are participating to protest actions taken by settlers against camp residents, for example.

While schools are the natural place for a demonstration to begin because of the large number of children gathered in one place, the current Palestinian uprising has managed to continue despite the fact that all schools and universities have been closed by Israeli military order. The current uprising has also spread beyond the refugee camps. In villages or cities, high strategic points or areas near the local mosques have become the launching points for most demonstrations. Entire communities have become involved in acts of resistance.

The size and shape of the refugee camps provide both an advantage and a disadvantage to the camp residents. On the one hand, the small area of the camp means that it can usually be controlled by only a few soldiers. But the proximity of homes and the network of alleys give an advantage to the youth, who know every corner and alley and who can use the roofs to move from house to house while soldiers search for them inside.

The situation is virtually the same in the old quarters of most cities. One advantage offered by the cities is the presence of high-rise buildings from which Palestinians can throw things down on the Israelis from a distance and then jump from one roof to another in order to escape. In villages, however, the situation is much different. Demonstrators have to take advantage of trees and rocky mountainsides. They often act as small teams that try to attack Israeli cars and stop soldiers or settlers from getting too close to the village.

Role Assignment

After watching numerous demonstrations, one can ascertain the assignment of tasks among the youth. The nature of the demonstrations forces on the different age groups a variety of roles. From Gaza to Nablus the distribution was consistent, though no formal communiques or statement in this regard were ever issued.

The youngest category of children involved in demonstrations is the seven-to-ten age group. Most of the time these children may be seen rolling tires to the middle of the road, pouring gasoline on them, and then setting them afire. The youngest are entrusted with this job for a number of reasons. Technically it is easy, but it is also one of the most important for the success of a particular stone-throwing incident. The burning of a tire prevents cars from traveling that particular road and, at the same time, the black smoke attracts soldiers. Since the children are under the legal age, their capture does not lead to prison term. At worst, they may be slapped around a bit and then released.

The eleven-to-fourteen age group is assigned the task of placing large stones in the road to slow down or stop traffic. This group has been seen in many places using homemade slings and slingshots. After the second month of the uprising, they could often be seen practicing with slings and competing amongst themselves to see who was the most skilled. The drawback of the slings and slingshots is that they can carry only a small stone, which at best will leave a mark in a passing car, but will not break the windshield.

untitled
Sliman Mansour-Palestinian

The young boy with paint brush in hand for paintng slogans on walls, a kaffiyeh around his neck, holds up the 'peace' gesture.

הלש   צוהלת   ושמחה

כמוני   מסכה   חא חא

חנוכה תשמ"ח

The fifteen-to-nineteen group comprises the veteran stone throwers. Normally masked with kafiyehs to hide their identity, this group can inflict the worst damage on passing cars. Using large rocks and standing relatively near the road, this group is the heart of the team. Consequently, they are the most sought after by the Israelis. However, their speed and knowledge of their turf give them a tremendous advantage over the soldiers, who are loaded down with equipment and who must travel in units so as not to be trapped. The young stone throwers are also given important responsibilities during curfews: they may be called upon to get food from outside the curfewed areas and to help in the distribution inside the areas.

Palestinians over age nineteen take key positions in order to lead the entire team. They are in contact with observers on the hillsides and on high houses and they help determine which cars are to be attacked and which are to be let go. They stand at an elevated point and direct the stone throwers as to when and how far to retreat when the soldiers advance. They decide on the moment of a countercharge, which is carried out with loud screams and a shower of stones. The leaders know the range of the Israeli weapons and are able to differentiate between rubber bullets and real bullets. When rubber bullets are used, the leaders scream, "Don't worry. They are shooting 'al fadi', which means roughly, "empty" or "blank". When the soldiers shoot real bullets, the leaders shout that the soldiers are firing 'al malan', meaning "full" or "the real thing". Even with real bullets, the leaders learn through experience the range of the various weapons being used. Leaders also seem to have the ability to determine whether soldiers plan to shoot in the air or at the demonstrators. Israeli newspapers have reported that one of the tactics used by the soldiers in trying to put down the demonstrations was to pick off the leaders using the Baretta sniper rifles.

The Unified National Command of the Uprising

Since its beginning on 9 December, the national uprising of Palestinians in the occupied territories has witnessed a dramatic shift from spontaneous protests to a more organized form of resistance. Without the disciplined organization that has evolved, the uprising, most experts believe, would have ended long ago. Commercial strikes, demonstrations, stone throwing, and blocking main roads with rocks, metal blocks, and burning tires continue to be the rule, rather than the exception, in most parts of the occupied territories.

These grassroots organizations took the form of labor unions, student councils, women's committees, and young people's social action committees.

The Beginnings of the Command

The curfews imposed by the Israelis in the first month of the uprising were one of the main factors that helped forge the unified local committees called "support committees". These committees were established without any specific idealogical bent but with the aim of providing food, milk, and medicine for the besieged camps. Committees based outside the curfewed areas were busy collecting food donations while the committees inside the curfewed areas took responsibility for distribution. Medical teams were also organized through the support committees to visit houses and attend to the sick in the curfewed areas. The idea was that if the camp residents were fed and well attended to, they could withstand the seige for a long time.

With the uprising now in its fourth month and with no end to occupation in sight the young stone throwers, the initiators of the uprising, seem unlikely to lay down their 'weapons.'

Happy New Year
David Tartakover-Israeli
1987

The poster was produced in 1987, the first year of the intifada. The Coca-Cola bottle appears as a Molotov cocktail, used by the fighters in the Intifada, but also used in the marketplaces to sell olive oil, a food staple of the country.

(opposite page)

Left/right-Boom!
Yarom Vardimon-Israeli
1992

The artist comments on the militaristic state of affairs in Israel.

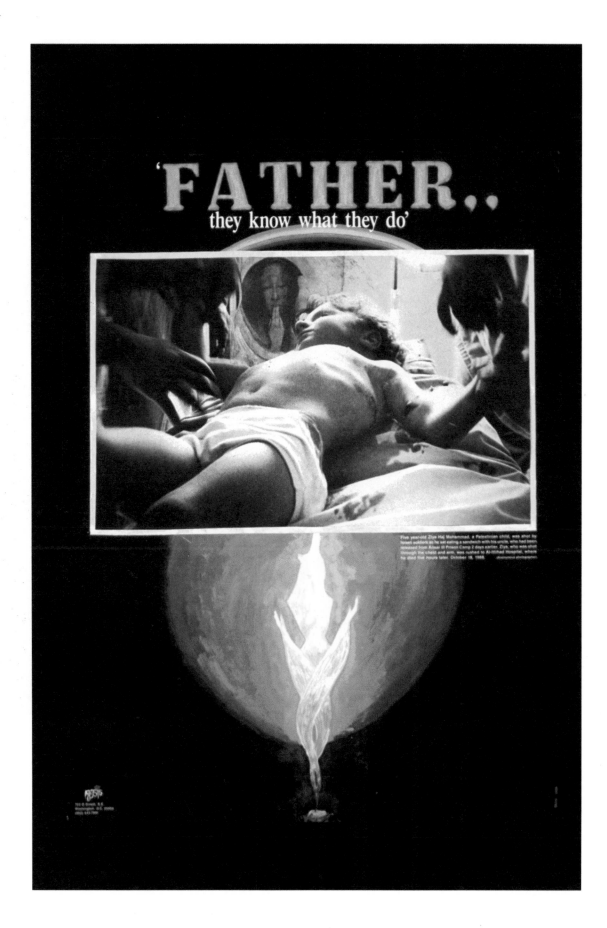

100

Yehuda Amichai

The Diameter of a Bomb

The diameter of the bomb was thirty centimeters
and the diameter of its effective range about seven meters,
with four dead and eleven wounded.
And around these, in a larger circle
of pain and time, two hospitals are scattered
and one graveyard. But the young woman
who was buried in the city she came from,
at a distance of more than a hundred kilometers,
enlarges the circle considerably,
and the solitary man mourning her death
at the distant shores of a country far across the sea
includes the entire world in the circle.
And I won't even mention the crying of orphans
that reaches up to the throne of God and
beyond, making
a circle with no end and no God.

Father, they know what they do
artist unknown-Palestinian
(from the collection of the Roots
Youth Organization, Washington D.C.)

The artist replaces the Biblical
words 'Father, forgive them;
they know not what they do' to
accuse the Israeli military as
well as the Israeli people of
being aware of the results of
their actions.

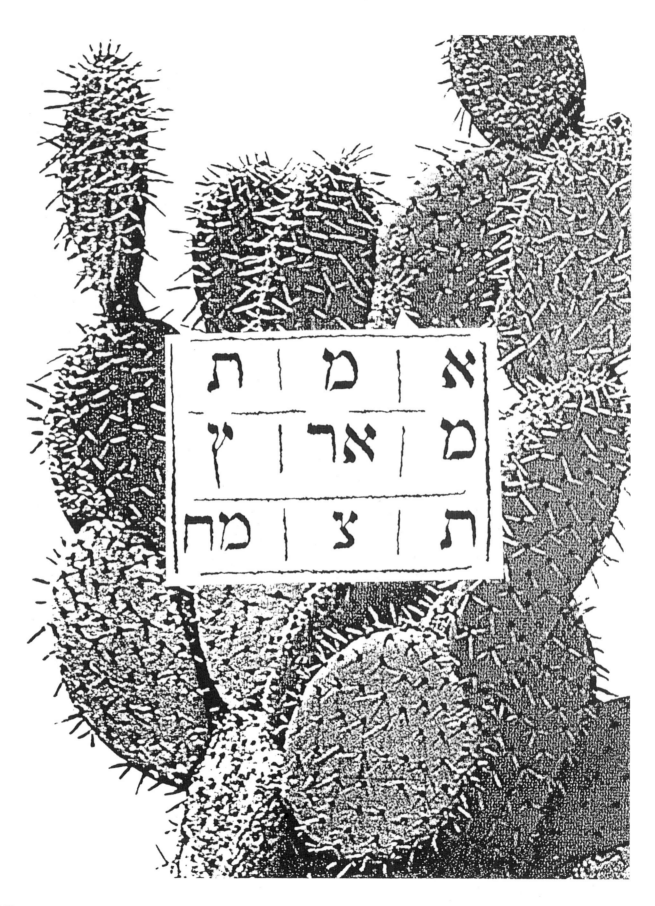

Administrative
David Tartakover-Israeli
1989

A poster created for a demonstration near the Ansar 3 Detention Camp, showing a bound Palestinian prisoner.

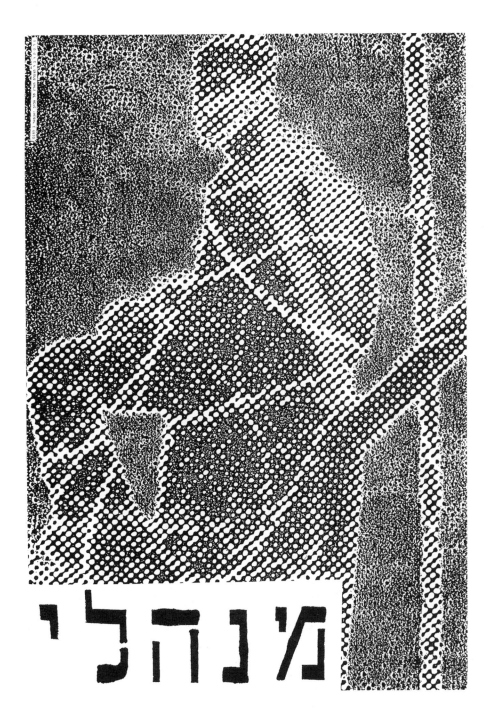

מנהלי

(opposite page)

And the Truth Shall Spring From the Earth
David Tartakover-Israeli

The sabra or cactus is symbolic of both native Israeli and Palestinian. The word 'truth' reads both from left to right and top to bottom.

Half full/half empty?
Ophir Paz-Israeli
1988

Paz produced this poster on the
occasion of Israel's 40th anniversary of independence in order
to question the state of affairs
in Israel after 40 years.

(opposite page)

Judaea Capta
Ilan Molcho-Israeli

The imprint on an old coin from
the times of Judaea takes on
new meaning: Are the Israelis
(Jews) the captors or the cap-
tees? The blood red Tree of
Lebanon in the background illus-
trates the question of the right
of Israel to invade Lebanon, an
unpopular war with the Israeli
people.

ואהבת לרעך כמוך

40 שנה לעצמאות ישראל

ישראל ה-40

Peace Now
Raphie Etgar-Israeli
1991

The poster says in Hebrew and Arabic, "Come give a hand to the chain of peace." The Jewish/Arabic Peace Chain was a peace rally in 1991 organized by Peace Now.

(opposite page)

Love thy neighbor as thyself
Ophir Paz-Israeli
1988

Produced for the 40th anniversary of Israel's independence.

25th Anniversary
unknown artist-Palestinian
(from the collection of Yale University
Library)

Produced by the FATEH faction
of the PLO, the poster cele-
brates its 25th anniversary.

Pray for the Peace of Jerusalem
Sabina Saad
1993

Produced for the Israel Information Center and the Ministry
of Education. The artist states
that the dark blue background
symbolizes the years of dark-
ness for the 2000 years the
Jews were in exile, and the section within the Star of David,
full of light, represents the
return of the Jews to a united
Jerusalem after the Six Day War.

2nd Anniversary
unknown artist-Palestinian
1989
(from the collection of Yale University
Library)

The torn Palestinian 'flag' over-
lays the desert full of stones
suggesting that the situation
has not improved much for the
Palestinians 2 years after their
uprising—the intifada.

Independence Day
Yossi Lemel-Israeli
1994

The traditional Jewish 'hammer'
used to playfully beat others on
New Years Day takes on new
meaning when painted in the
colors of the Palestinian flag.

One of Us
Yossi Lemel-Israeli

A play by Beni Barabash about
the investigation of one soldier
accused by another of killing a
Palestinian prisoner.

And the sons have returned to
their country
David Tartakover-Israeli
1996

Tartakover reproduced an old
poster from an Israeli youth
organization and added the
green line which demarcates the
land between Israel and the
Occupied Territories. The text
could be applied to Palestinians
today.

עזה כמוות

18.5.94 צה"ל מפנה את רצועת עזה

**Israel's 40th Anniversary
Iris Dishon-Israeli
1988**

Produced for the 40th anniversary of Israeli independence, the image is based on a famous photograph of Theodor Hertzl in Basel, Switzerland, in 1897, where he predicted the establishment of a Jewish homeland. Here, the artist replaced Hertzl with Arafat, contemplating a similar idea.

(opposite page)

**It's Noble to Die for
Our Country
Arie Berliner-Israeli
1994**

Berliner, while a student at the Bezalel Academy of Art and Design in Jerusalem, created this poster using the words spoken by the national hero Yosef Trumpeldor who fought against the Arabs in the 1920's. The artist uses the colors of the Palestinian flag to express the same words.

Ahmad Dahbour

The Camel of Burdens

Ahmad Dahbour is a poet with a
deeply felt understanding of the
Palestinian situation. His eight
collections of poetry to date include
The Story of the Palestinian Boy
(1979), *Mixing Night and Day*
(1979), and *Twenty-One Seas*
(1980). Dahbour is also the Deputy
Minister of Culture in Gaza.

Oh, you camel of burdens,
our road is thorny
and only your teeth can grind the thorns.
Our road is full of sand, but you are the sailor and the runner.
In our childhood, we memorized
your name in our reading books.
You were the ship of the desert.
On the days we hovered on the edge of despair,
you came trembling like children
emerging through the pains of labor,
you came from the parched throat
and the air of the poor.
Oh, you camel of burdens,
walk on with us.
Emulating the grass
we shall not complain.
Some of us will scorch under the hot sun.
Some will be killed when the thorns are thick,
some when death is a spear
parting the road.
But emulating the grass,
we shall not complain.
When the time arrives
that the arch of Haifa shades our eyes,
our ancient hunger shall release
our imprisoned tears.
Oh, camel of burdens, walk with us,
and when we arrive, say to us, "Cry."
For all great happiness has its sorrow
and sadness is one of the fruits of joy.

Carry On
Sliman Mansour-Palestinian

An Arab refugee carries Jerusalem on his back. The poster, a
reproduction of a painting, was
a very popular poster in Palestinian households. Jerusalem
has been central in the conflict
as to whom the city belongs:
the Palestinians want their portion returned. The painting was
inspired by the poem 'The
Camel of Burdens' by Ahmad
Dahbour.

(translated by Aziz Shihab & Naomi Shihab Nye)

אין אלוהים מלבד בגין
ובגין נביאו!

"יאל קומרן" אחרי נאמה

איקרית "צליבת-האדמה"

Igael Tumarkin

Three Times Arrabeh

Igael Tumarkin immigrated to Palestine from Germany where he had worked with Bertoldt Brecht as a stage designer. In Israel he has worked as an artist—painting, printmaking and creating well over a 100 outdoor sculptures all over the world. He has received many awards including the Rodin Grand Prize, Japan, 1992.

The Israel Lands Administration certainly won't give you an olive tree for your sculpture, right? So try and talk an Arab fellow into letting you have one. Tell him nothing will happen to his tree, and he'll be free to pick its olives. Go tell a fellow you want to define an olive tree and create an environment aspiring to a symbol, even to peace. Go tell him that you, too, firmly respect the sanctity of the tree and of the land it grows on. You've no intention of marking out a military firing range, nor putting up a settlement, and if you do send in a bulldozer it will only be to plough and harrow a patch around a tree, 10 meters in diameter, no more. Go and find yourself a fellow who'll lend you an olive tree.

I go on the road—talking, persuading—to Galilee. It's winter, rain, cold.

Maybe I should try: If you don't like it—your money back, and the olive'll still be yours. Just a bit of junk, some earth, a few stones. A 20th Century *maqahm*, if you like, an altar, a sacred tree, and a statement we're both interested in. You ask, and so does he: "Does an Arab understand art?" Well, does a Jew? We're all of this place and understand the symbols of this place. Of then, of now. This is the code: tree, earth, sun, and the wind of Galilee.

At last there's one who consents to give up a tree and a patch of ground. Only temporarily, but still. It's at the Lotem Junction. Military Firing Range No. 9. The absurdity of it: they say—rocky terrain, unworkable, the Arabs don't need it, and next they plough it, and sow, and then declare: "See, Jews are making the Galilee bloom." Firing Range Nine Plus Observation Post, 1980. Splendid. You can't help thinking: Jews are building themselves concentration camps, isolated, fenced in like crusader forts. Whoever wounds the land- the land will thrust him out.

Now I have an olive tree, I create an environment. An hour's ploughing at a 10 meter diameter. A pair of man-high stakes of earth, staking out a claim. A traditional seat of mortared brick surrounded by tin boards painted silver.

I call it an "ejection seat" to myself. It isolates the viewer from his surroundings, lets him concentrate on the earth pillars and olive-tree landscape. Is coexistence possible, I ask. You answer, the tractor ploughs, and the symbols rise. Youngsters come and help, disparaging at first, then it begins shaping up. The seat is fixed, heaped up for the *maqahm*. I must remember the rule I've made myself- to touch: touch the landscape, not force it, not turn it about too much. To define a tree in the landscape by symbols, create "a place." Water basins—there should always be water, and a place to bury weapons. Weapons must be turned into scrap, roots, dry twigs. "Indians, bury your tomahawks."

Then there's a sunset and pictures are taken.

Two days later the sculpture is demolished by a person or persons unknown.

**Crucifiction
Igael Tumarkin-Israeli**

Tumarkin created outdoor sculptures around Israel and Palestine, many with social and political messages. The poster shows Tumarkin in front of one of his sculptures.

117

الشهيدُ الفنان ناجي العلي

Naji al-Ali
artist unknown-Palestinian
(from the collection of Anne Marie
Oliver and Paul Steinberg)

Naji al-Ali, an influential and
well known Palestinian cartoon-
ist, created the figure of the
child witness 'Handala,' which is
often seen on the walls of
refugee camps as a figure of
lost innocence and mute
reproach. Though popular for
his cartoons pillorying Israel
and America, his bold attacks
on the established Arab political
structure won him his greatest
following. He was assassinated
in London on August 29, 1987.

'Handala'

(opposite page)

2nd Anniversary of the Intifada
artist unknown-Palestinian
(from the Yale University Library
Collection)

The fist, raised in defiance
through the Star of David
(made of barbed wire typically
found surrounding refugee
camps and areas forbidden for
entry for Palestinians), is holding a stone, symbolic of the
shebab or stone throwers

2ND ANNIVERSARY
OF THE PALESTINIAN „INTIFADA"

Al Aqsa Day
Taysir Batniji-Palestinian
1990

On October 8, 1990, Moslems
went to pray at the Dome of the
Rock (Al Aqsa) in Jerusalem.
There was a clash between
Moslems and the Israeli military
which resulted in 20 Palestinian
dead and 400 injured. It is
known as the Al Aqsa Massacre.
The poster is an original painting and collage.

(opposite page)

Step Forward
Wesam A'abed-Palestinian
1990

The bare foot, representing the
impoverished state of the
Palestinians, is taking a 'step
forward' into the future with
determination to 'crush under
foot' the Israeli military, which
the artist suggests by the red
river of blood, is responsible for
spilling the blood of Palestinians. The poster is an original
painting and collage.

Igael Tumarkin

Jericho, Twelve Years Later

A deserted refugee camp, rain-soaked, muddy, wind-racked, battered and bleak, a child's shoe.

A child. A picture: a child in Warsaw Ghetto, a child in Vietnam, a child at Avivim, a child in Lebanon. I take a picture of a child's shoe. Scorching sun and moaning wind. High noon. I am a refugee too: an exile from hope. Zionism was a dream, but the reality is a tragedy.
1979.

How are you? I ask a boy at Nahalein—"So long as you are well, I am ill. My home there has been blown up by your brethren."

**International Day of the Child
Taysir Batniji-Palestinian
1990**

To commemorate the Day of the Child, Batniji shows the prison bars to remind us of the children in refugee camps which he indicates are 'faceless' to their imprisoners.

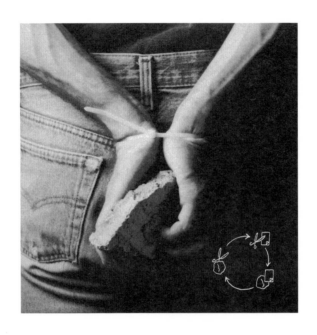

Stone, Paper, Scissors-Triptych
Ilan Molcho-Israeli
(from the collection of the Judaica
Division of the Harvard College
Library)

The child's game 'Scissors, paper,
stone' takes on new meaning in
the image of a Palestinian prisoner.

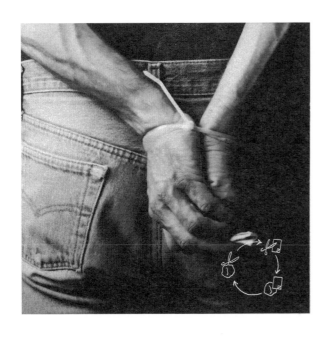

Ahmad Dahbour

The Price of a Cup of Tea

This is a book of my hopes
To drink the tea at dawn,
leaving the city its buried treasures
and writing to the one who shared
the wound of my departure
To make this real
I need, first of all,
the city of my soul
And what is it?
Time and safe land
Memories and a street
What? Is this too much?
Am I dissatisfied?
Has the sun set on the earth
and the sea retreated
that I have no land or ship?
All for the sake of a cup of tea,
a notebook,
and stamps.
I must have slingshots,
and soldiers,
and cannons.

(translated by Aziz Shihab & Naomi Shihab Nye)

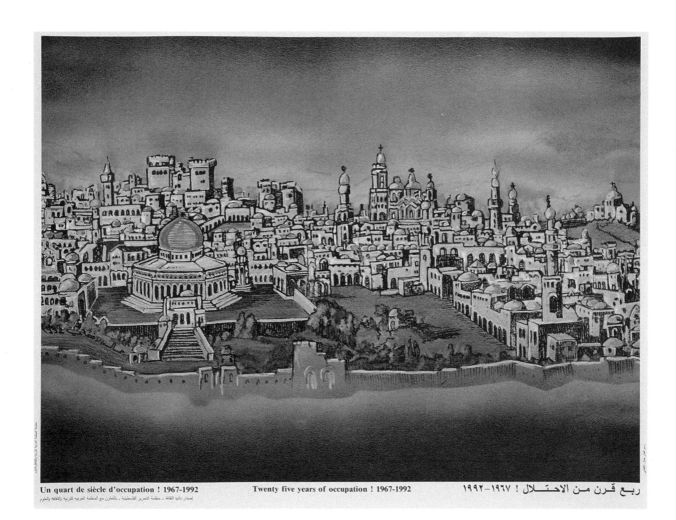

Un quart de siècle d'occupation ! 1967-1992   Twenty five years of occupation ! 1967-1992   ربع قرن مـن الاحـتـلال ! ١٩٦٧–١٩٩٢

إصدار دائرة الثقافة – منظمة التحرير الفلسطينية – بالتعاون مع المنظمة العربية للتربية والثقافة والعلوم

**25 Years of Occupation—
1967-1992
Jamal Afghani-Palestinian
1992**

The painting—Jerusalem with
the Dome of the Rock prominent in the foreground—refers
to the Six Day War, which
resulted in the Israelis taking
over the Palestinian section of
Jerusalem.

Alphabet
Arik Lichtman- Israeli
1990

This is a reaction poster to the Intifada with names of both Arab and Jewish children listed alphabetically. Without the typically Arab and Jewish names, the children would not be differentiated.

(opposite page)

The Mother of All Wars
Gali Hos-Israeli
1991

The artists gives literal expression to the term used for the Gulf War.

this is a real alarm. due to a missile attack on israel
all residents must put on gas masks
and enter the sealed room immediately.

6-year-old Jonathan made a gas mask for his teddy.
Now. neither of them are afraid.

Raja Shehadeh

The Sealed Room

17 January 1991

9:30 a.m. I was in a deep sleep when the telephone rang. Someone was trying to wake me up to tell me what I did not want to hear. The ringing would not stop. I left my bed and walked to the telephone and picked it up. It was Mark Taylor, Penny's colleague at the University. "I'm phoning to let you know the war has started," he said. It was 2:30 a.m.

I walked back to the room. What we dreaded had come. We could hear both our upstairs and downstairs neighbors moving furniture. It sounded as though they were moving big pieces. Were they barricading themselves in? Should we?

I began moving from room to room, systematically closing all metal shutters and window frames. Then I heard the door open across the hall and looking out saw Mustafa at the top of the stairs looking pale, a cigarette dangling from his lips. He was just leaving to go to Jerusalem to the Union of Medical Relief Committees which he heads. We looked at each other and nodded, but said nothing.

After I had closed all the windows and doors, I began stuffing newspapers into the cracks. With every room that I finished, I felt I was increasing the distance between us and the outside which I expected soon to be contaminated with deadly fumes. Penny was running to and from the kitchen, bringing basic foodstuffs into the room. I filled the bath in case the water gets cut off and then went back to my door. There were still cracks to stuff but Penny said, "Leave that now and let's finish the sealing."

We went into my study—the room we had chosen for sealing—and closed the door behind us. I wondered how long it would be before we opened the door again. Penny turned on the radio. She taped one side of one of the two windows in the room and I taped the other side. I looked through the light transparent plastic sheet we were using to protect ourselves and saw a hole in the plastic which I quickly taped over. Perhaps our plastic roll was not such a bargain, after all.

We turned on the television and heard the Israeli announcer telling everyone to keep their gas-masks handy. We waited, huddled together under our quilt. There was silence all around us. Our neighbors must have already sealed themselves into their own respective worlds.

There wasn't much to do now but wait. No news was coming from Iraq. How was it that they were not resisting their attackers? The last we heard was a dubbed version of Saddam's 'mother of all battles' speech, invoking Islam and Palestine. Will he prove himself the fool instead of the hero?

Raja Shehadeh—lawyer, lecturer, and founder and co-director of Al-Haq, an organization devoted to promoting the understanding and observance of the rule of law and the legal protection of human rights—has written many articles concerning the ideals of Al-Haq. He received the Rothko Chapel Award for Commitment to Truth and Freedom and acted as legal advisor to the Palestinian Delegation to the Israeli-Palestinian Peace Talks in Washington D.C. 1991-92. He continues to lecture extensively on the legal and human rights aspects of the Israeli-Palestinian conflict.

Jonathan's Teddy Bear
Eytan Hendel-Israeli
1990

During the Gulf War, Israelis and Palestinians were under constant alert of chemical attack from the Iraqis. A child draws a gas mask for his 'teddy.'

In the Arabic broadcast on Israeli radio there were no instructions for those without gas-masks, only news that strict curfew has been imposed and any resistance will be severely crushed.

As we waited under our rose-colored quilt, I reflected that all the very bad news that I had ever got in my life had come over the telephone, waking me up from deep sleep. How will I ever forget the telephone call about my father's murder. The telephone rang and rang in that determined way it does when someone is calling to wake you up however long it takes. How I hate telephones!

Penny had fixed her mind on a seven o'clock deadline. She thought that if we had not been hit by then, we would be OK. The long night would be over.

The seven o'clock Israeli-English television news had Defence Minister Moshe Arens pronouncing it a very good morning indeed. He announced with unconcealed glee the on-the-ground destruction of all Iraqi missiles. A dream come true.

It is now mid-morning and we are all confused. What did Saddam have in mind? Why did he refuse to compromise? What defences did he have and why did he not use them? How will the world treat our case after this?

I am glad that I did some work yesterday and that we managed to release the al-Haq statement to the press about the failure to distrubute gas-masks and the danger to which the thousands of detainees who are in detention centers near army camps, living in tents without any protection, are exposed.

I just got a call from the foreign researchers who are at the London office of al-Haq. We spoke at length. We were cut off three times. I am glad they are there; they may be more useful outside than here.

It's unclear what kind of human-rights work we will be able to do. The main issue now is the lack of protection for the Palestinain population on even the most elementary level of an air-raid siren. The possible wartime scenarios of expulsions and massacres weigh heavily on my mind.

Fateh telephoned from Vera's.

"I slept until six this morning," he said. "I suppose most people heard by telephone that the war had started. But those, like me, who don't have a telephone may as well have been at the North pole. I'm furious. I've been trying to get a telephone for a year and a half. And yesterday when I heard that they were distributing gas-masks, I walked over to the military headquarters. People were falling over each other; I couldn't even get to the door. The army distributed a few masks and sent us all away. I could have been poisoned in my sleep. There isn't even a siren to wake me up. The only way to hear of a raid, is to keep the radio on day and night. I'll go carzy by the end of the war. I can't tell you how angry I am."

On Your Face
Yossi Lemel-Israeli
1990

Printed six months before the Gulf War, this poster, titled 'On Your Face'—slang for a 'lousy situation'—predicts the situation during the Gulf War when the people of Tel Aviv were under attack by Iraq and feared chemical war. The gas mask straps are in the shape of the Star of David.

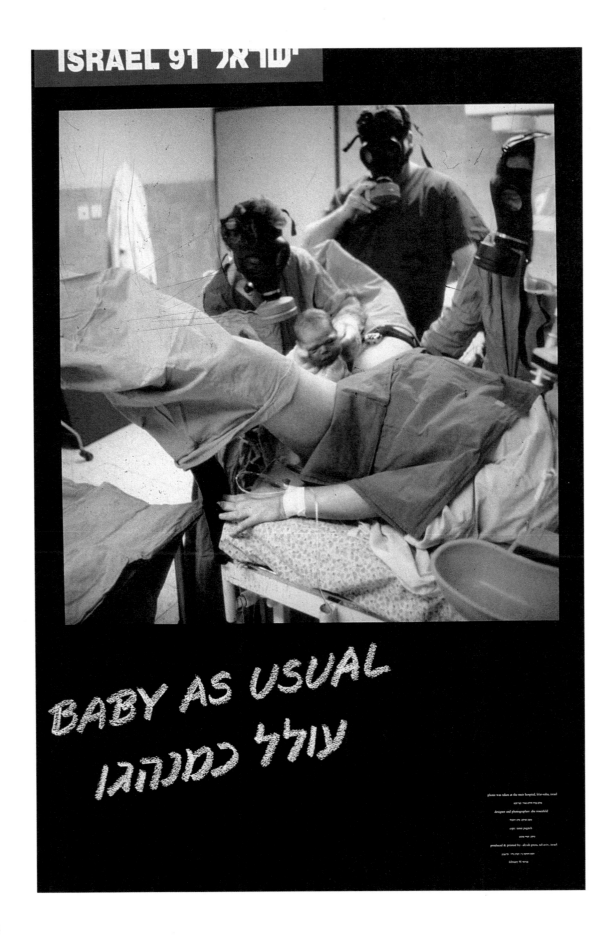

All this is typical. For their people the Israeli authorities cater superbly. When it comes to our side everything is always done deliberately badly. Just imagine, no announcement that masks are being distributed, no word about where the distribution stations are to be found. If you are 'well-connected', you may be able to find out and may be able to get a gas-mask. Otherwise you really don't stand a chance. Even if you manage to get to the right place at the right time, the distribution takes place in a disorganized manner and you cannot be sure that if you respect the queue you will succeed. So you push and shove and if you are fortunate and aggressive, you make it. Then your new mask is without instructions and no one tells you how to use it. 'You wanted one? Take it. Here it is.' And, of course, it comes without the atropine shots—and to say the least, it's given begrudgingly.

Fateh also expressed his disillusion with Arab leaders, 'A repeat performance, he called it, much talk and no action. Much bravado before the battle begins, then no resistance. Like Abdel Nasser, like Assad, like Saddam. With such leaders we are doomed. As long as the Arab individual isn't liberated, it's going to be useless. Without democracy and freedom we will never stand a chance.'

I still hear the planes overhead. They have not stopped since war was declared. Bahia, my aunt, just phoned. She said that her household followed all the instructions about the sealing of the room, including the placing of towels dipped in bleach at the base of the door. Her eldest son is in Jericho. It must be the worst place because it lies at such a low level that the clouds of chemicals will settle there, and because it is so close to the border that if there are going to be explosions the Jericho residents will be the first out.

I appreciated Bahia's call. In the absence of a central authority, we have to take care of each other. Communal solidarity and mutual support is all and everything. In the absence of a siren we shall continue to depend on the telephone call of friends to warn us. Pity we don't have a telephone in our sealed room.

You cannot store electricity so I don't worry about conserving it but it is the water I worry about. I emptied the water in the bath into buckets. I was comforted to learn last week that the Ramallah water works company is the same authority that serves military camps and Jewish settlements. The authorities will not cut off their water so we should be all right as long as it doesn't become contaminated. I wonder how long we will be able to make international calls. They may be banned as they were for most of 1988 at the beginning of our homegrown war, the Intifada.

Baby as Usual
Abe Rosenfeld-Israeli
1991

A normal delivery, except for the gas masks, the artist indicates that in Israel, under constant fear of attack, life must and does continue even under duress.

Two Symbols. One Message
Roger Cook-American/Palestinian
1996

The artist invites individual
interpretation of the combining
of two powerful symbols, the
Star of David and the American
flag.

The Kaffiyah Speaks its Peace
Roger Cook-American/Palestinian
1996

The artist has taken the Arab
kaffiyah headdress (often associated by western audiences with
'terrorist' groups) and juxtaposed
the western peace symbol on
pins in the colors of the Palestinian flag, indicating the Palestinians' desire for peace.

The Back of the Mountain
Ilan Molcho-Israeli

The Back of the Mountain refers to Jordan, symbolized by the red and white kaffiyah (a black and white usually represents the Palestinian people) which until the recent peace treaty had no communication with Israel, but kept a watchful eye.

(opposite page)

Peace Process
Ilan Molcho-Israeli

The artist presents a cynical view of the peace process. Two men identical except for a 'kaffiyah' (a traditional head scarf worn by Palestinian men) to differentiate the two, stand at a urinal expressing the same sentiment.

139

Revolution Until Victory
artist unknown-Palestinian
1981
(from the collection of Roots
Palestinian Youth Organization,
Washington D.C.)

Produced by the PLO for their
16th anniversary, the 'candle' is
made of a gun around which the
Palestinian flag swirls.

(opposite page)

No to Chaos. Yes to Dialog.
Sliman Mansour-Palestinian
1995

The artist is calling to his fellow
Palestinians to stop using arms
against each other.

142

Anne Marie Oliver and Paul Steinberg

The Other Side of Peace

Anne Marie Oliver and Paul
Steinberg are writers based in
Cambridge, MA and since 1993,
have been Visiting Scholars at The
Center for Middle Eastern Studies,
Harvard University. Of the six yaers
they spent in Israel, the West Bank,
and the Gaza Strip, they lived for
half a year in Khan Yunis, Gaza,
with a Palestinian refugee family.
From 1990-93, they were researchers at the Truman Institute for the
Advancement of Peace, The Hebrew University of Jerusalem, and
from 1991-93, their work on the
intifada and the Israeli-Palestinian
conflict was supported by The
Harry Frank Guggenheim Foundation. Their work has appeared in
many publications including *The
Jerusalem Report* and the International Journal of Comparative-
Sociology. They have lectured extensively around the country and
their forthcoming book focuses on
the suicide squadrons of Hamas
(University of Oxford Press).

Islam is the Solution
artist unknown-Palestinian
(from the collection of Anne Marie
Oliver and Paul Steinberg)

Under the byword "Islam is the
solution" an artist has depicted
an avenging Islamic eagle as it
frees the Dome of the Rock, the
most contested site in the Arab/
Israeli conflict, from the tentacles
of an octopus, a primary symbol
of a global Jewish/Masonic con-
spiracy in the media of Hamas.
The figure owes its origins to
western anti-Semitic works, as
well as the revoluionary art of
Iran whose influence became
more prominent in the artwork of
Hamas after the Israeli government expelled 400 of the movement's leaders to an Iranian-influ-
enced Shi'a stronghold in south
Lebanon in 1992. "Jerusalem/
Palestine" is written at the bottom of the poster as an assertion
of owhership of the city and its
sacred sites

The most capable and prolific propagandist of the myriad factions active in the West Bank and Gaza Strip during the intifada was the Islamic Resistance Movement (IRM), best known by its acronym, Hamas. Aiming for the 'ideological mobilization' and renewal of the Palestinian populace, the organization devoted considerable time and care to the pro- duction of 'Islamic art', which it defines in the nineteenth subject of its covenant as some- thing which "awakens movement and excites the soul to lofty heights and sound con- duct." The aims of Islamic art, according to the document, are opposed to those of 'un- Islamic art': "Man is an exceedingly wondrous creation made from a handful of mud and a puff of breath, and Islamic art addresses man on this basis, while an un-Islamic art addresses the body and favors the mud." Inspired by the movements call, Hamas devo- tees produced media as diverse as audiocassettes and videotapes, plays and leaflets, graf- fiti and murals, prison newspapers and martyr cards. Most of this media was illegal dur- ing the Israeli occupation of the territories and remain so today under the Palestinian National Authority.

Less ephemeral than graffiti and less permanent than videotape were the posters and can- vases which filled funeral tents, public squares, and mosques throughout the Bank and Strip during the uprising. Although some were printed on underground presses, many posters were simply Xeroxed drawings, often taped together to form long banners. When more time was available, Hamas artists created elaborate canvases, making do with what- ever materials could be had—bed sheets and house paint, newspaper clippings and flourescent Hi-liters, or, as in the examples featured here in "Both Sides of Peace," poster board and crayon. Whatever their media, Hamas artists visualized elemental themes and long-standing obsessions—power and justice, suffering and revenge, martyrdom and apocalyptic yearning. Most of the underground art of the Hamas is one-dimensional, for- mulaic, even cartoonish. Even the simplest calligrammatic figures recalling ancient Arabic techniques of writing are not exempt from the tendency towards kitsch, as when the Hamas byword "The intifada continues" is formed from blood spilling from the back of a boy-martyr, or the identifying marker 'Hamas' is spelled out with mosques, skulls, and Kalishnikovs.

Many images are emblems which taken together, form an allegorical system in which fidelity is celebrated and infidelity denounced and punished; others are violent images which possess an immediate correspondence with contemporary events. A Ship of Salvation sails across a stormy sea; blood drips from a golden sun onto the sacred precincts of the Dome of the Rock; an oil lamp burns and never runs dry. An opened Qur'an, bracketed between crisscrossed rifles. An Hamas ghost rears its head above a sleeping Israeli soldier, who wakes in terror and runs, screaming for his mother. A tree is hung with the dead bodies of Israeli soldiers, as if with Christmas ornaments, or is root- ed in the ground hallowed by the sun-bleached bones of dead Palestinian fighters. A fire- breathing dragon encircles the globe in a pythonic squeeze. Red poppies sprout from land irrigated with the blood of martyrs. An exploded bus smolders on a road littered with broken bodies. A bomb detonates in a shower of apocalyptic orange, a foreshadowing of the End of the World.

The intifada heralded the end of one world and the beginning of another. A major challenge of the time was the creation of images which captured this transformation, reproduced it in the hearts and minds of the Palestinians, moving them from anger and disappointment to resistance, protest and action. Hamas answered this challenge with grandiose if often ineloquent icons of pain and ecstacy, unity and dismemberment, inflation and collapse, command and obedience, sacrifice and transcendence. In its most Boschian tableaux can be seen the desperate attempts of a movement to substantiate itself and its ideology with the indisputable reality of flesh and blood.

untitled
artist unknown-Palestinian
1987
(from the collection of Anne Marie Oliver and Paul Steinberg)

Long time staples of Palestinian folklore, trees possess intense political import for Palestinians. The olive tree represents perpetuity and connection with the land and the orange tree of dispossession. This original poster was produced by the HAMAS.

(opposite page)

Amnesty
Fadal Timraz-Palestinian

Calling for amnesty of Palestinian political prisoners held in Israeli prisons, the original hand-painted poster was made by artist Timraz who lives in the Der Elbalah Refugee Camp north of Gaza City.

Jihad-Wake Up Israel!
artist unknown-Israeli
1996

A right wing poster showing
Arafat in a Nazi helmet, suggesting anti-Semitism.

The Liar
artist unknown-Israeli
1996
(from the collection of Anne Marie Oliver and
Paul Steinberg)

The peace talks have revealed a wide
gap in Israeli society, between those
who feel that territorial losses in
exchange for peace with the Arabs are
risks worth taking and those who
assert that such risks will lead to further war and destruction. A product
from the latter group, this poster
depicts late Prime Minister Yitzhak
Rabin dressed in Yasir Arafat's checkered kaffiyah (which many Israelis still
equate with terrorism). At the top of
the poster is written 'Liar' and at the
bottom 'Elections Now!' After the assassination of Rabin in November 1995,
many Israelis blamed this sort of
rhetoric and imagery for creating the
climate that made such an action possible.

זה לא שלום.
THIS IS NOT PEACE.

יום העצמאות 1995

This is Not Peace
artist unknown-Israeli
1996

This poster was produced by a
right wing political party stating
its view of the peace process.
The Star of David made with a
dove is the logo for the Israeli
Tourism Bureau, but in this
poster, the dove is shot dead.

**"...and most important-The Land
of Israel"**
Rami & Jacky-Israeli
1984

In the style of Soviet propaganda posters and reminiscent of
the young communist pioneers
who first settled in Palestine,
this poster was produced for the
right wing political parties-
Tehiya-Tzomet.

untitled
artist unknown-Palestinian

A popular street poster found in
Gaza contains all the icons of
Palestinian nationalism: The
Dome of the Rock (Al Aqsa), the
Moslem mosque in Jerusalem;
Palestinian President Arafat, and
doves painted in the colors of
the Palestinian flag.

(opposite page)

**With Participation, Results will
Happen**
artist unknown-Palestinian
1996

A typical poster found on the
streets in Gaza produced by the
Palestinian National Authority to
promote voting in the first elec-
tion in the Occupied Territories.
Yasir Arafat was elected
President.

GAZA 15 _ 22 JULY 1993

The Exhibition -Supported By YMCA -Gaza

أقيم هذا المعرض برعاية جمعية الشبان المسيحيه – غزة .

150

Fawzy El Emrany

The Ivory Beam

The canvas isn't prepared yet—
The crowded drawings on the walls
which suffer from pain
Neither are ready
to meet the ivory beam...
The embroidered beam with soft edges

Only the green olive branch
stands against the club
and the tyrant bullet
it cannot stop the gunshot
aimed at the core of the eye...

Then I picked up my paint brush
and wandered along
the edges of my broken dreams.

Fawzy El Emrany, artist and art teacher from Gaza, has had several one-man exhibitions in Gaza, the West Bank, Jerusalem and Europe. He is co-curator for the exhibition "Both Sides of Peace" and is studying for his Masters Degree in Art at the Art Academy in Halle, Germany.

Peace for the World and for Us
Taysir Batniji, Fawzy El Emrany
and Fayez Sirsawi-Palestinian
1993

Created for an art exhibition of works promoting the peace process, Batniji and El Emrany use Arabic typography.

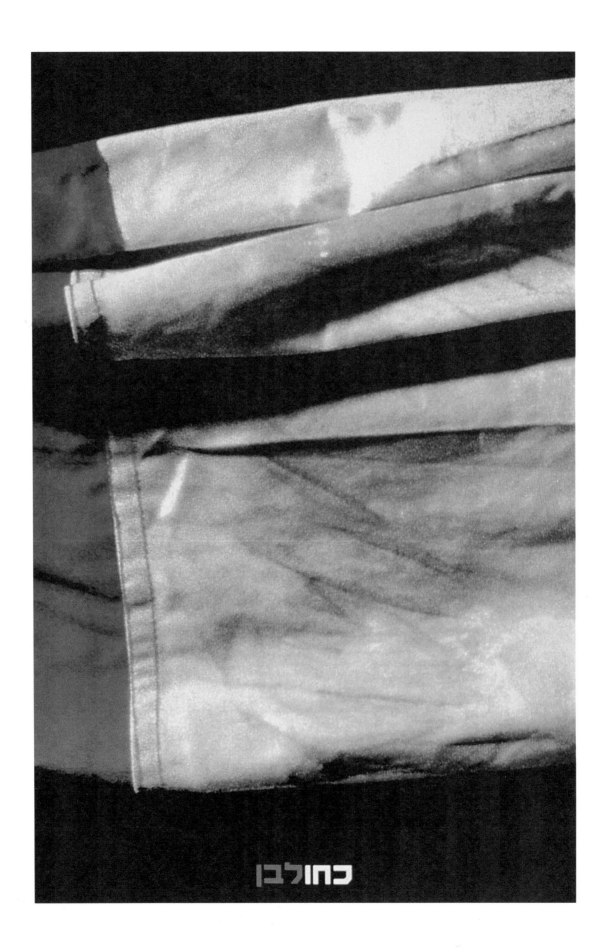

כחולבן

Peace
Raphie Etgar-Israeli
1996

This peace poster was produced for the Israeli Ministry of the Interior.

(opposite page)

Blue White
Raphie Etgar-Israeli
1995

Etgar shows a portion of the Israeli flag, often referred to as the 'blue white.' His comment on the state of internal affairs is made by showing a soiled flag. The artist noted that he produced this poster, which received sharp criticism from the Israeli right-wing, just days before Prime Minister Rabin was assassinated, adding sad poignancy to the poster.

Peace by Piece
Tamar Kelner-Israeli
1996

The green and black olives,
representing the two peoples
of Israel and Palestine, placed
together to form the olive
branch of peace.

(opposite page)

untitled
Yarom Vardimon-Israeli

The artist combines the symbols
of war and peace indicating a
contradictory 'peace process.'

ثلاثون عاماً على الانطلاقة

30ᵗʰ ANNIVERSARY OF THE PALESTINIAN REVOLUTION

**30th Anniversary of the
Palestinian Revolution
artist unknown-Palestinian
1995**

A poster found plastered on a
wall in Ramallah, the West Bank.

Nora Whisnant

Timeline

1516
Palestine becomes a province of the
Ottoman Empire until 1918.

1882-1891
The first large immigration (*aliyah*)
of primarily Russian Jews to
Palestine occurs. By 1891 Arabs in
Jerusalem request the Ottoman
Government to prohibit Jewish
immigration and purchase of land.

1896
Hertzl writes *The Jewish State*, carrying the inspiration for Zionism
(the call for a Jewish homeland)
to German Jews.

1905-1914
The second large emigration of
European Jews occurs. By 1911
organized Arab opposition to
Jewish settlements is evident.

1914
World War I begins and Jews support Germany, Austria-Hungary
and the Ottoman Empire . Approximately 700,000 people live in
Palestine of which 9-12% are Jews.

1917
The Balfour Declaration: Britain's
Foreign Secretary, Lord Balfour
endorses the formation of a Jewish
State in Palestine but pledges not to
harm the "existing non-Jewish
communities."

1918
World War I ends. The Anglo-
French Declaration states that
Arabs of the former Ottoman
empire shall have their independence as a reward for supporting
the allies: Palestinian Arabs are
excluded. Britain's Egyptian
Expeditionary Force and Faysal's
Arab Army jointly occupy
Palestine. The provisional government becomes embroiled in the
struggle between Jewish settlers
hastening in to form their new state
and Arab inhabitants and neighbors who resist.

1921-22
Britain sets up the Emmirate of
Transjordan, which removes from
Palestine two-thirds of the land east

of the Jordan River. The League of Nations awards Britain the Palestine Mandate and charges them with carrying out the Balfour Declaration.

1933-1936
Massive immigration of Jews escaping Nazis begins. By 1936, Jews comprise 28% of the population. Palestinian Arabs, concerned about their lands and rights and inspired by other Arab nationalist movements, rebel by attacking Jewish settlements and British military units.

1939-1946
World War II begins and many Jews join the Allies. As the Nazi threat recedes, militant Zionist groups such as Irgun (headed by Menachem Begin), turn to violent acts against Britain including assassinations. By 1946, Jews comprise 32% of the population.

1947
UN General Assembly calls for a Partition Plan for Palestine giving Jews approximately 54% of the land of Palestine. All five UN Arab countries oppose the plan. The lands to be given are still about half Arab inhabited. Attacks on Palestinian villages and Jewish settlements increase. Most Palestinians flee.

1948
Israel declares its independence and defeats the armies of Egypt, Syria, Lebanon, Transjordan and Iraq which send soldiers to join local Palestinian Arabs resisting the establishment of the Jewish State. Approximately 150,000 Palestinians remain in Israel and about 750,000 dispossessed Palestinians crowd refugee camps in Egypt (Gaza), Jordan (West Bank), Syria and Lebanon.

1956
Israel joins Britain and France in their attack of Egypt resulting in Israel's occupation of most of the Sinai Peninsula. (Israel later withdraws under pressure from the United States and the United Nations.)

1964
The Palestine Liberation Organization (PLO) is formed by Arab heads of state in Cairo, Egypt. The PLO is to act as the central organization for civic and paramilitary

groups serving Palestinain Arabs. Palestinian representatives led by Ahmad Al Shuquayri appoint an executive board and adopt a national charter calling for a Palestinian State within the British Mandate borders.

1967
The Six Days War: in preemptive air strikes, Israel defeats Egypt, Jordan and Syria, and expands its territory to occupy the Gaza Strip, the Sinai Peninsula, the West Bank and the Golan Heights - thereby acquiring over a million Palestinians. Over the next two years approximately 7,600 Arab houses are destroyed; by 1971 the number more than doubles. Conditions in the overcrowded refugee camps deteriorate over the next 20 years as the population more than doubles.

1969-1970
Yasir Arafat (leader of the al Fatah faction) is elected Chairman of the Executive Committee of the PLO. Although Arafat leads the largest group of guerrilla fighters (freedom fighters—fedayeen) extremists groups such as the Popular Front for the Liberation of Palestine (PFLP) led by George Habash are at times more visible via hijackings, etc. Jordanian military and Palestinian guerrilla forces clash, many Palestinian civilians are killed (Black September 1970)

1974-1976
Arab heads of state name the PLO the sole legitimate representative of the Palestinian people and elections in the Occupied Territories 2 years later confirm Palestinian support for the PLO. The United Nations invites Arafat to speak at the General Assembly, adopts a resolution recognizing Palestinians' right to nationhood and grants the PLO observer status.

1977-1979
Egyptian President Anwar Sadat visits Jerusalem offering peace in exchange for Israeli withdrawal from Sinai. In the 1978 Camp David Accords, President Carter, Prime Minister Begin and President Sadat draft a peace treaty which is signed in 1979. Sadat is assassinated in 1981.

1982
Israel invades Lebanon and is involved in the massacre of hundreds of Palestinian civilians in the Sabra and Shatila refugee camps by allied Phalangist militia. The defeated PLO withdraws to Tunis. Israel withdraws from most of Lebanon in 1985.

1987
The intifada: In Gaza, Palestinian youths spontaneously revolt against the occupying Israeli army. The uprising spreads to the other Occupied areas. During the next seven years over 2,000 Palestinians are killed; 25,000 wounded, and about 130,000 are imprisoned; 219 Israeli soldiers and civilians die.

1988
The Palestinian National Council (PNC), a 'parliament' in exile, declares Palestine a State. Yasir Arafat publicly recognizes Israel-opening the doors to negotiations for peace.

1990-1991
The Gulf War: Iraq invades and occupies Kuwait. The PLO voices support for Iraq. Led by the United States, a coalition of American , European and Arab countries send forces and arms to Saudi Arabia in Operation Desert Storm. Massive air and ground attacks force Iraq's withdrawal from Kuwait. Palestinians flee retributions in Kuwait resulting in hundreds of thousands of refugees in Jordanian refugee camps. At the Madrid Conference, Arab (including Palestinians) and Israeli delegates meet to discuss the Middle East situation, water rights etc. Dissolution of the USSR leaves the United States as the main superpower affecting Middle East policies.

1993
Secret negotiations in Oslo, Norway lead to the signing of the Declaration of Principles which offer autonomy to Palestinians in Gaza, Jericho and eventually the remainder of the West Bank. Prime Minister Rabin shakes hands with Chairman Arafat on the White House lawn.

1994-1997
Extremists in both camps attempt to derail the peace initiatives. In

the 1994 Hebron massacre 29 Muslim worshippers are killed by a Jewish zealot. Palestinian militants begin a rash of suicide bombings in Israel. In 1995, Prime Minister Rabin is assassinated by an Israeli extremist. Yasir Arafat is elected President of the Palestinian Authority. In 1996 Benjamin Netanyahu, outspoken critic of Rabin and the peace negotiations, is elected prime Minister. Building of new Israeli settlements in Arab Jerusalem escalates, further jeopardizing the peace process.

Sources:
Frankel, G. *Beyond the Promised Land: Jews and Arabs on the Road to a New Israel*, Simon & Schuster, New York 1996
Friedman, T. *From Beirut to Jerusalem*, Farrar Straus Giroux, New York 1989
Goldschmidt, A. *A Concise History of the Middle East*, Westview Press, CO 1996
Said, E. *The Question of Palestine*, Vintage Books, New York 1992.
The World Book Encyclopedia, Chicago, 1982

אמייא

Mother
David Tartakover-Israeli

An Israeli soldier on patrol in
the Territories may be thinking
of his mother as he passes an
Arab woman, and she, perhaps,
of her son.

Permissions

Gratitude is extended to the authors and artists and publishers for permission to reprint all the material in this book.

Excerpts from THE YELLOW WIND by David Grossman, translated by Haim Watzman. Translation ©1988 by Haim Watzman. Reprinted by permission of Farrar, Straus & Giroux and Random House UK Ltd. (for UK and Commonwealth).

'Two Hearts' by Glenn Frankel. Reprinted by permission of Simon & Schuster from BEYOND THE PROMISED LAND by Glenn Frankel. Copyright ©1994 by Glenn Frankel. Afterward copyright ©1996 by Glenn Frankel.

'My Enemy My Self' and 'Second Thoughts' by Yorum Binur. Excerpts from MY ENEMY MY SELF by Yorum Binur are reprinted by permission of Doubleday, a division of Bantam Doubleday Dell Publishing Group, Inc.

Excerpt from BROKEN BRIDGE by Lynne Reid Banks reprinted by permission of Morrow Junior Books, a division of William Morrow & Co., Inc. Copyright © 1993 by Lynne Reid Banks.

'Letter from Gaza', 'Umm Saad', and 'a letter to his son' reprinted by permission of Lynne Reinner Publishers, Inc. from MEN IN THE SUN by Ghassan Kanafani.

'At the Bridge' by Amos Oz reprinted by permission of Harcourt Brace Publishers.

All other material reprinted by permission of the authors and artists.

Colophon

The concept, design, production and editing of this book by Dana Bartelt, New Orleans, LA, Text layout design by Maria Rogal, Gainesville, FL, and Dana Bartelt. Editing assistance by Nora Whisnant, Princeton, NJ, Sara Lemel, Tel Aviv, Israel, and Glenn Frankel, Washington D.C.. Proofreading by Carol Leake, New Orleans, LA. Photographs of the posters by Greg Plachta Photography, Durham, NC and David Simonton, Raleigh, NC. Scanning by Eyebeam, Morrisville, NC. Translations by Sara and Yossi Lemel, Sliman Mansour, Fawzy El Emrany, Nabil Mohamad, Aziz Shihab, and Naomi Shihab Nye. Electronic composition in Berkeley and Meta. Printing by Meredith Webb, Burlington, NC. Paper by Gilbert Paper—Esse® White Smooth 80# Cover and 80# Text. Cover design by Yossi Lemel, and cover photograph by Israel Cohen, Tel Aviv, Israel.

Printed in North Carolina.